The Power of
IMAGINATION

Shippensburg, PA

The Power of
IMAGINATION

Unlocking
Your Ability
to Receive
from God

Andrew Wommack

The Power of Imagination

Unlocking Your Ability to Receive from God

ISBN: 978-1-68031-286-7

Ebook: 978-1-68031-287-4

LP: 978-1-68031-288-1

HC: 978-1-68031-289-8

Copyright © 2019 by Andrew Wommack Ministries Inc.

Published by Harrison House Publishers, Shippensburg, PA 17257
www.harrisonhouse.com

CONTENTS

INTRODUCTION

Imagination is the dynamo, the power source of life. But most people don't understand its importance. They don't understand that God built imagination into our makeup. Psalm 103:14 says:

> *For he knoweth our frame; he remembereth that*
> *we are dust.*

The same Hebrew word that was translated *"frame"* in this verse was translated *"imagination"* or *"imaginations"* five times in the Old Testament (Gen. 6:5, 8:21; Deut. 31:21; 1 Chr. 28:9, and 29:18). Our imagination is the frame or spine of our existence. It's the doorway to our potential and affects the way we view life (Prov. 23:7). But people relegate imagination to the realm of childhood fantasy. They underestimate its influence in their lives and try to receive from God without first activating their imaginations.

When Jamie and I started out in ministry, the Lord gave us a vision of reaching multitudes—of touching people all over the world. And though we knew that this was God's will for our lives, there was very little evidence suggesting it would come to pass. People stayed away from our meetings by the thousands. We struggled to find traction. It was frustrating. Then, in 2002, the Lord spoke to me from Psalm 78 and told me I was limiting Him by my small thinking. You see, even though I knew God's will for my life, I could not see myself doing it. I couldn't see myself standing in front of thousands of people or influencing millions on television. I couldn't imagine people speaking my name in the same breath as other ministers who had impacted the world. And because I couldn't see it, I didn't. The Lord showed me that in order to fulfill His will for my life, I had to change the way I thought. I had to start using my imagination.

Your imagination is like your spiritual womb. It's your creative center. Genesis 11 records the account of the tower of Babel. As the ancient population grew and began spreading out upon the earth, the people gathered on the plains of Babylon. There, they devised a plan to make a name for themselves (Gen. 11:4) and to reach heaven.

> *And the L*ORD *came down to see the city and the tower, which the children of men builded. And the* L*ORD said, Behold, the people is one, and they have all one language; and this they begin to do: and now nothing will be restrained from them, which they have **imagined** to do.*
>
> **Genesis 11:5-6, emphasis added**

That's amazing! The imagination of this unregenerate people so threatened God's plan for mankind, He had to put a stumbling block in front of them—by dividing their language—to slow them down and give His plan time to work out. God saw their imagination as a threat to His plan for man. Wow!

Imagination is powerful. It is the first step in doing. If you can imagine something, you can do it. Yet many Christians don't understand this. Believers all over the world pray for healing and never experience it. They pray for prosperity but never receive it. Why? Because they don't know how to use a godly, positive imagination. They don't see themselves healed. They don't see themselves prosperous.

If you want to see God's will for your life come to pass, if you want to reach your full potential, you need to understand both the power of your imagination and the correct way to use it.

Chapter 1

WHAT IS IMAGINATION?

According to the *Houghton Mifflin American Heritage Electronic Dictionary*, the word *imagination* means "the process or power of forming a mental image of something not real or present." Many people confuse imagination with vision. But vision is "a mental image produced by the imagination" (*HMAHED*). You can't have vision without an imagination. And while these words might be used interchangeably sometimes, I want to focus on imagination—the ability to see what isn't present.

Most adults associate imagination with childishness. They've been taught that using their imagination or believing in something they cannot see is fantasy. This same dictionary calls fantasy an "illusion" or "a delusion," a "whimsical notion," or "a daydream." Just look at the definition of the word *delusion*:

"a false belief held in spite of invalidating evidence." Fantasy isn't real. It isn't based on validating evidence. But imagination is real.

Imagination is the ability to see with the mind what you cannot see with the eyes. If I were to ask you how many windows were in your childhood home, I bet you'd know, even though you probably never counted them. Thanks to your imagination, your mind's eye can recreate your childhood home and walk you through it room by room.

Whether you realize it or not, you use your imagination every day. You use it to remember where you parked your car or to give someone directions. You can't live without imagination. If I were to say the word *dog* to you, you wouldn't picture the letters D-O-G in your mind. Instead, your mind would bring up a picture of a dog. If you owned a little white dog, that's probably the picture you would see. But I could change your picture with my words. If I said the words *big black dog*, your picture would change.

Imagination helps you "see" what can't be seen. It creates the pictures in your mind that help you remember, read, and plan. But imagination can only work with the information you give it—good or bad, right or wrong (Luke 6:45). If you fill your imagination with the garbage of this world, that's what it will produce. But if you renew your mind to the truth of the Word, your imagination will help you receive from God (Rom. 12:2).

If I had the space, I could go through almost every main character in the Bible and show how each one used their imagination to receive from God. When the Lord spoke to Abram (before his name was changed to Abraham) in Genesis, God told him to leave his father's house and go to a land he would later inherit (Gen. 12:1). Abram couldn't see the land God spoke of; he didn't know from experience that it would be a good land. As far as we know, he'd never traveled any farther than Haran (Gen. 11:31). So, why did Abram leave everything he knew? I believe it was because the Lord's words engaged his imagination.

Abram's imagination was essential in his ability to receive from God—and thus become Abraham. And so is yours. You cannot accidentally accomplish God's will for your life. A while back, I received an email from a lady who works at one of our Bible college campuses. She was praising the Lord and thanking me, saying, "I was made for what I'm doing. This is exactly where God wants me to be." Sadly, most people can't say that. They don't know God's will for their lives. They don't have a vision—a mental image—of their future. They're like water, just going with the flow, following the path of least resistance. But any old fish, even a dead one, can float downstream.

When the Lord spoke to Abram and told him to go, Abram didn't know where he was going. He didn't know what life would look like outside Haran, but he started out anyway. Abram had a vision of a better inheritance than what Ur or Haran could provide, and as he sought the Lord, Abram's imagination began working. As he traveled the land, Abram saw himself owning it. He saw his descendants living there. His imagination produced a vision that became clearer and clearer the farther he got from Ur.

I believe this is why the Lord gave Abraham the promise that his seed would be as numerous as *"the dust of the earth"* (Gen. 13:16) and *"the stars"* (Gen. 15:5). Every day Abraham had dust on his feet, and every night he looked at the stars. These things kept God's promise constantly in front of him and helped quicken his imagination.

Abraham's vision was like a roadmap for his life. Think of it. If you were traveling from Colorado to New York, you'd want a map—an idea or picture of where you were going. Without one, any old road would do. But not any old road will get you where you want to go in life.

Most Christians don't have a clear vision for their lives. They cannot see God's will. But instead of seeking the Lord and engaging their imaginations like Abraham did, they let the circumstances of life push them around. They leave a good church and the support system of friends and family to move cross-country for a hundred-dollar raise. They spend thousands on medicines that help them cope with sickness and disease. They mortgage their future to buy boats they won't use and extra televisions they don't need. They settle for less than God's best.

Proverbs 29:18 says, *"Where there is no vision, the people perish."* Vision, or the image produced in your imagination, gives you hope for the future. Without it, you'll never fulfill God's plan for your life. Circumstances will divert you, hardship will steal from you, and you'll quit. In the fifty years since God called Jamie and me into the ministry, there have been many opportunities for us to quit. We've dealt with poverty and slander and have lost relationships, but vision kept us going. When I was spit on and threatened at gunpoint, when people lied about me, when people called the ministry a cult, it would have been easy to say, "This isn't worth the effort." Instead, I let my vision motivate me. I encouraged myself by focusing on what God told me to do, and now it's paying off!

A person's vision will sustain them when everything around them seems contrary.

Do you have a vision—a hope-filled picture of the future? Does that picture match God's picture for you? The good news is, regardless of the decisions you've made or how far off course you find yourself, God is better than any GPS system. If you've made a wrong turn or gotten off track, He can get you back on. But you'll need the power of your imagination.

Chapter 2

THE MISSING LINK

Your imagination is responsible for creating the roadmap that your life follows. Whether you realize it or not, your life is exactly the way you've imagined it to be. Proverbs 23:7 says that as a man *"thinketh in his heart, so is he."* If you see yourself poor, no matter how many zeros are on your paycheck, your wallet will always experience more month than money. If you feel victimized or oppressed, there will always be some person or circumstance keeping you from reaching your goals. You may know that God wants you well and prosperous (3 John 2). You may even be praying for it. But if you can't see yourself as God sees you, you'll never experience His best.

Years ago, a woman came to work for us who'd been abused by her husband. Though she'd gotten out of that situation, she feared men—all men. In her mind, men were evil, and they couldn't be trusted. To her, everything men did was an attempt to gain control or manipulate her. This woman let the circumstances of her past paint a distorted picture of reality. And she filtered every interaction through that picture. Her imagination was out of control, and it cost her dearly.

Your imagination is the dominant controlling factor in your life. It works like a governor on a car. Some vehicles have built-in safety features called governors. A governor controls a car's speed. Once a driver hits the speed limit set on their car, the governor kicks in to restrict the amount of air and fuel the engine receives. No matter what a driver does, they can't go above that limit. Your imagination works the same way. But unlike a car, the Manufacturer does not set your imagination's limits. You do.

A good friend of mine grew up under a mean, angry father. Living under his father's roof was oppressive. He told me once how his dad used cars for parts. They probably had fifty junk cars parked on their farm at any given time, and his dad would take parts out of one to repair something else. Every time my friend helped repair the cars, his dad would say, "You're so stupid! You can't screw a nut on a bolt."

After years of hearing that message, it became a self-fulfilling prophecy in my friend's life. I remember working with him on a car years later. And as smart and capable as my friend was, I'd watch him shake every time he had to put a nut on a bolt, terrified he'd cross-thread it. One time my friend had put the nut on just fine, but he was so afraid he'd cross-threaded it, he took the nut off and put it on again. He kept doing it until he eventually cross-threaded that bolt. To this day, I've never seen my friend put a nut on a bolt that wasn't cross-threaded. His dad's words painted an image in his mind that limited what he could do.

You may not realize it, but you filter everything—who you are, what you can do, your circumstances, even the way you've been treated—through your imagination. And that imagination, if not properly directed, limits what God can do in your life.

My mother was a schoolteacher. She loved education and always made a big deal of our academic achievements. When I was in sixth grade, my brother took a test that tagged his IQ at genius level. When I heard my mother talking about his results, I asked about my score. She said I was "two points above an idiot." Years later she laughed about that day, saying, "That's not true, Andy. I must have been joking with you." But I never knew it was a joke. Her words, spoken in jest, painted a picture of mediocrity in my mind that I struggled with for years. It wasn't until the Lord revealed spirit, soul, and body to me that my imagination began to change.

Before I understood the concept of spirit, soul, and body, my reflection in the mirror was the only "me" I knew. Others' opinions and my own feelings drove my life. I didn't realize that the real me—my spirit—was the part of me created in God's image (Gen. 1:26).

And the very God of peace sanctify you wholly; and
I pray God your whole spirit and soul and body be

> *preserved blameless unto the coming of our Lord
> Jesus Christ.*

1 Thessalonians 5:23

We cannot see, hear, or feel our spirits with our five senses
(1 Cor. 2:14). There's only one way to understand what spirit is:
to look into the Word of God.

> *For the word of God is quick, and powerful, and
> sharper than any twoedged sword, piercing even
> to the dividing asunder of soul and spirit, and of
> the joints and marrow, and is a discerner of the
> thoughts and intents of the heart.*

Hebrews 4:12

God's Word shows us spiritual truth. Jesus said, *"It is the
spirit that quickeneth; the flesh profiteth nothing: the words that I
speak unto you, they are spirit, and they are life"* (John 6:63).

As I began to dig into the Word as a young man, I discovered that *"he that is joined unto the Lord is one spirit"* (1 Cor.
6:17) and *"as* [Jesus] *is, so are we in this world"* (1 John 4:17,
brackets added). I began to realize that my spirit was identical
to Jesus's spirit and that I could do the same things He did
(John 14:12). God's Word began changing my internal picture, and as that picture changed, so did I. Instead of seeing an
introvert in the mirror, I saw Jesus living in me. I didn't see a
man with a little bit of Jesus's nature and a little bit of my own.

I saw a man God-possessed—someone complete and powerful, able to heal the sick, raise the dead, and use the authority Christ had given him (Mark 16:17-18).

Once I saw those things in my imagination, it was only a matter of time before I began seeing them in my life. Since then, I've seen the dead raised, blind eyes and deaf ears opened, people healed of cancers, and others walk out of wheelchairs. I've seen all sorts of miracles. My own son was raised from the dead. All of these things happened because the Word of God painted a different picture in my imagination.

Many people want to see the miraculous. They want to experience God's best and see Him work in their lives, but they do not see themselves as God sees them. In their minds, they limit themselves to only being human. They spend their lives coping with allergies, worrying about the stock market, and fearing every report they see on the "ten spies" network. They expect to get sick. They expect to grow old and lose their eyesight.

But as believers, we are not only human! Our physical bodies may be mortal, our minds may still be corruptible, but we are new creatures in Christ Jesus (2 Cor. 5:17). The same Spirit that raised Christ from the dead is living in us. In our spirits, we are pure and holy, full of God's power. One-third of us is wall-to-wall Holy Ghost (Rom. 8:11)! And if we choose to believe it, our spirits will dominate, trumping what goes on in the physical realm. But we first need to change our imaginations.

Years ago, John G. Lake, a well-known healing minister in the early 1900s, told a story of his experience in South Africa during an outbreak of bubonic plague. People were getting sick and dying like flies, but no one would bury the dead. Everyone was terrified of contracting the deadly disease—everyone except Lake.

Lake worked diligently during the plague, burying multiple people a day, until a British ship with supplies and doctors finally arrived. After watching Lake, one of the doctors asked him how he'd been protecting himself from infection. Lake replied that the law of the Spirit of life in Christ Jesus was his protection and that no germ would ever attach itself to him.

Not many people would say that. They simply cannot see it. But Lake did. When he declared that no germ could touch his body and live, the doctors laughed. They didn't believe him. So, Lake proposed a test. He told a doctor to collect spit from one of the dead and put it under a microscope. As expected, live germs covered the slide. Lake suggested they put those germs in his hands and look again. The doctors did, and what they saw astonished them. When the germs touched Lake's skin, they died!

Did you know that this same power is promised to every believer? Psalm 91:10 says:

> *There shall no evil befall thee, neither shall any plague come nigh thy dwelling.*

Anyone who believes the promises of Psalm 91 and confesses them in faith (Ps. 91:2) can have the same protection from plagues that John G. Lake had, but most Christians never experience these kinds of results, because they are more impressed by what they hear on the news than what they hear from the pulpit. They're more moved by what their doctor says than by what God says. Instead of their inner image coming from the light of God's Word, it comes from the light of a television set. Most Christians limit themselves to the world's experience. They do not let the Word of God change their imaginations.

When the Lord spoke to me in 2002 (shortly after the terrorist attacks on the Twin Towers) and told me I was limiting Him, I called my staff together and said, "I don't know how long it takes to change this image on the inside, but I am going to change. I am going to do what God called me to do." Though everything in the natural screamed that expanding during such a time was impossible, I was shocked at how quickly our ministry began prospering.

During this time, no one was watching Christian television. No one was giving to Christian ministries. Everyone's attention was drawn to the news. Every television ministry I knew of suffered. Parachurch ministries slashed their budgets. Then, without warning—before I could get anything out to my partners, before I could do anything but change my imagination—our income doubled. It was like there was a dam in the spiritual realm holding back all the blessings God wanted to get to me. God was providing. He was faithfully performing His Word. But something had stopped up the flow. When I turned on my imagination and changed my internal image, that dam broke. And just like Deuteronomy 28:2 promises, a flood of God's provision overtook me.

You can read more about my personal experience with changing my imagination in my book *Don't Limit God*.

Chapter 3

NARROW-MINDEDNESS

This concept of imagination should not be foreign territory for Christians. We deal in "things unseen" all the time. We believe in a God and a heaven we've never seen. We stake our eternity on the words of an ancient book. And we believe that a Man we've never met paid the price for our sin 2,000 years before we were even born! To the natural mind, this sounds crazy, yet it's true.

I was listening to the radio recently and heard a talk show host discussing a moral issue with his audience. One of his listeners called in to counter what was being said. "The Bible says—" the listener began, but the show's host interrupted, "We aren't dealing in the Bible. We're dealing with reality. We don't want any ideas or beliefs. We want reality." I got so mad, I started yelling at the radio, "The Bible is more real than anything you can see, taste, hear, smell, or feel!" The physical world, what most people refer to as "reality," was created by the spiritual. Hebrews says:

> *Through faith we understand that the worlds were framed by the word of God, so that things which are seen were not made of things which do appear.*
>
> **Hebrews 11:3**

The Word of God created everything we can see with our physical eyes. The Word is real, but it's not a reality that can be experienced with our natural senses (1 Cor. 2:14). It cannot be seen with our eyes or touched with our hands. It, like the rest of the spiritual world, must be experienced by faith.

During the "Great Recession" in 2008, when stock prices went down 50 percent and the housing market crashed, the Lord spoke to me about building a world-class Charis Bible College campus. Since that time, we've purchased and begun development on 493 pristine mountain acres in Woodland Park, Colorado. We've spent over $70 million above my normal expenses building a 70,000-square-foot building called The Barn to house our Charis classrooms and a 140,000-square-foot building that includes a 3,200-seat auditorium, our phone center, and our Charis offices. And we have renovated another 60,000-square-foot building on the property for our AWM offices and television studio. All of this was done debt-free.

While everyone else was struggling and just barely getting by during the "Great Recession," we were prospering. We were building. There's no natural explanation for this. We didn't take out a loan or tap into investor funds. We didn't have a huge amount of savings to draw from. All we had was God's Word. We let the Word of God paint a picture of what was possible, of what we could do, and that picture has become so clear and so strong that we can no longer live outside it. We've become narrow-minded in pursuit of God's will!

You see, faith and imagination work hand in hand. You can get so focused, so narrow-minded, on Scripture that you can't see anything contrary to it. That's a positive thing!

Years ago, my board sent me to the doctor for a stress test. (The insurance policy we were applying for required one.) As the doctor began prepping me for the treadmill, his nurse asked if they could shave the hair off my chest to give the electrodes a place to stick. "You can't shave my chest," I said. "This is virgin hair. It's never been touched!" They honored my request and tried to stick those things to my chest without shaving it, but about thirteen minutes into the test, they started falling off. In order to finish, I had to hold two electrodes in place, the nurse held two, and the doctor held two more. When I finished running, the doctor looked over my results. Then he started grunting and writing on my chart. When he finally looked up at me, he said, "Here's the name of a doctor I know. He's a specialist. I want you to go over there and get tested right away. We may admit you into the hospital for open-heart surgery before the day is over."

I was shocked! I didn't feel ill. The only reason I went to see the doctor was for that insurance policy. How could I need open-heart surgery? As I sat there for a second looking at the doctor, I began thinking about the image of health and strength God's Word had painted inside me. And I said to him, "That's a lie. I don't believe it. You look at that readout again and tell me that it says I have a heart problem."

The doctor just looked at me (I guess he wasn't used to people calling him a liar) and said, "Well, it doesn't really say you have a heart problem. It just says that there was an abnormality during testing. It may be nothing, but it could be something serious. We need to get you tested." He didn't think about the fact that those electrodes were falling off my chest! "That's not what you told me," I said, getting mad. "You told me I might have to have open-heart surgery before the day is over. You lied to me!"

"Fine," he said, tearing up the paper. "You're on your own; get out of here."

Later that day, on my way home, a woman's car died. It was blocking the road, so I got out and pushed it to the nearest pull-off. I pushed it up the hill and around the corner—by myself. Not bad for a guy who was supposed to have open-heart surgery that same day!

My point is, the Word of God has the power to change what you see. My dad died when I was twelve years old. He had heart problems. He actually died twice, once in 1952 and again in 1962. The first time he died, the hospital pronounced him dead, covered him with a sheet, and put him on a gurney in the hall. It was about two o'clock in the morning. Our pastor back home was leading an all-night prayer meeting for him. At the same moment the male orderly came to push my father down to the morgue, our pastor stood up back home and said, "Either God has done what He said and healed him, or he's dead. Either way, I'm done praying; I'm going home." Next thing anyone knew, my dad was raised from the dead. He kicked off his sheet, and the orderly wet his pants right in the middle of the hospital corridor! Because of my dad's heart issues, every time I go in for a checkup, the doctors start projecting his problems onto me.

I could behave like the rest of the world, giving those words weight. I could let the doctors' words intimidate me and influence the way I see myself. Instead, I stand on the Word of God that says Jesus purchased my healing at Calvary (1 Pet. 2:24). I trust that God's Word is flawless, that He is *"a shield unto them that put their trust in him"* (Prov. 30:5) and that no plague can come nigh my dwelling (Ps. 91:10). I believe that *"the joy of the LORD is* [my] *strength"* (Neh. 8:10, brackets added). I encourage myself with scriptural examples like Moses, who, on the day he died at 120 years old, climbed Mount Nebo. The Bible says that *"his eye was not dim, nor his natural force abated"* (Deut. 34:7). I break the doctors' curse by saying, "Fifty percent of me is my mother. She lived to be ninety-six and was as healthy as a horse. Why don't you look at her side?" At the time of this writing, I've outlived my dad by more than fifteen years. And according to my last nuclear stress test, I have the heart of a teenager!

After the doctor in Colorado Springs flunked me, my friend (a doctor on my board) invited me down to his place in Louisiana for a nuclear stress test. He said, "Those treadmill tests are wrong 50 percent of the time. Never base a health decision on one of those tests." So, they injected me with some kind of dye and took pictures of my heart at rest and after exercise. My friend told me, "There's nothing wrong with you. You have the heart of a seventeen-year-old."

Brothers and sisters, you don't have to let your genes, your education, or your past dictate your future! Give yourself permission to become narrow-minded in the Word. Change your imagination.

Chapter 4

DEVELOPING
A PICTURE

And be not conformed to this world: but be ye transformed by the renewing of your mind, that ye may prove what is that good, and acceptable, and perfect, will of God.

Romans 12:2

Developing a godly, positive imagination is a huge part of mind renewal, and it's often the part that trips people up. Though this concept is simple, it's not easy. There is no "quick fix" for your imagination. A godly imagination can't be given by the laying on of hands. *You* have to choose to change. But changing the way you think and see is a process. It takes time and consistency. I've been working on it for decades, and while I've certainly not arrived, thank God I've left!

Years ago, I decided I didn't want to live my life like the ten spies who went with Joshua and Caleb to spy out the Promised Land. In Numbers, before the children of Israel entered Canaan, Moses sent representatives from each of the tribes to scout out the area. He specifically asked them to investigate the land's terrain and fertileness, the type of people who lived there, and the size and strength of its cities (Num. 13:17-20). When the spies returned, they brought back evidence of God's provision—a hunk of grapes so huge, it had to be carried between two men! But they also brought this report:

> *And they told him, and said, We came unto the land whither thou sentest us, and surely it floweth with milk and honey; and this is the fruit of it. Nevertheless the people be strong that dwell in the land, and the cities are walled, and very great: and moreover we saw the children of Anak there.*
>
> **Numbers 13:27-28**

Canaan was a bountiful land, more so than the children of Israel dreamed was possible. But instead of believing God's Word, they let circumstances push them off course. Though Caleb tried to encourage them, the people couldn't see beyond the giants:

> *But the men that went up with him said, We be not able to go up against the people; for they are*

stronger than we. And they brought up an evil report of the land which they had searched unto the children of Israel, saying, The land, through which we have gone to search it, is a land that eateth up the inhabitants thereof; and all the people that we saw in it are men of a great stature. And there we saw the giants, the sons of Anak, which come of the giants: and we were in our own sight as grasshoppers, and so we were in their sight.

Numbers 13:31-33

The fact that giants lived in the land of Canaan didn't negate the Israelites' ability to conquer it. Their imaginations kept them from inheriting God's promise. They allowed the words of ten men—*"we were in our own sight as grasshoppers"*—to change the way they saw themselves and limit how much of God's will they could accomplish.

Forty years later, when Joshua sent two spies into Jericho, they found out that the Canaanites' hearts had melted and their might had departed the day they heard about the Israelites' miraculous crossing of the Red Sea (Josh. 2:9-11). If the Israelites had invaded then, it would have been a cakewalk. Their enemy's strength was gone. Instead, the Israelites were defeated in their imaginations. They saw themselves as grasshoppers (Num. 13:33). That was the problem.

Years later, when David fought Goliath, he had the same opportunity to be defeated by his imagination. And just like before, this battle between Israel and the giants of the land wasn't going to be a fair fight. But this time, the outcome was different!

> *And as* [David] *talked with* [his brothers], *behold, there came up the champion, the Philistine of Gath, Goliath by name, out of the armies of the Philistines, and spake according to the same words: and David heard them. And all the men of Israel, when they saw the man, fled from him, and were sore afraid.*
>
> **1 Samuel 17:23-24, brackets added**

> *And David spake to the men that stood by him, saying, What shall be done to the man that killeth this Philistine, and taketh away the reproach from Israel?* **for who is this uncircumcised Philistine,** *that he should defy the armies of the living God?*
>
> **1 Samuel 17:26, emphasis added**

Instead of seeing himself as a grasshopper, David saw himself according to his covenant with God. He knew that Goliath, a man outside that covenant, didn't stand a chance.

That's the way we ought to be. When cancer or poverty or fear comes knocking, our faith should shout, "Who do you think you are, coming against me, a child of the Most High?

I'm going to destroy you and rub your nose in defeat. You will rue the day you ever messed with me!"

Unfortunately, most of us would not dare speak like that. We don't see ourselves as the Word depicts us or as God sees us. That's the reason we're stuck under the circumstances. We see ourselves as grasshoppers—small, weak, and poor. We see ourselves as victims. But we are not victims! Almighty God lives in us! We should expect different results.

When I read the story of David and Goliath as a kid, long before I understood the importance of imagination, I remember going outside and marking the tree in my backyard at the height Goliath was. I made another mark at the height David was and bent down trying to imagine the battle from his perspective. Years later, when Jamie and I were visiting Israel, our tour bus stopped in the Valley of Elah, where David fought Goliath. It was a hot day, but our guide told us where we were and asked if anyone wanted to get out. No one did. Everyone wanted to stay in the air-conditioned bus—everyone except me. Thankfully, the rest of our group was gracious enough to let me go exploring, so I hopped off the bus and walked down into the valley. The Valley of Elah is about four miles across. I hiked down to a dry streambed that ran through the middle of the valley and picked up five smooth stones. As I stood there looking out over the hills, I imagined the Philistines positioned on one side and the Israelites on the other. I saw Goliath standing on the ridge and imagined David coming up behind his brothers as Goliath shouted, "Is there not a man who will fight me?" I watched the Israelites cower in fear, and I felt David's righteous indignation. The whole story came alive that day, replaying itself on those hills—not because I could see it with my physical eyes, but because I experienced it in my imagination. You see, there's no special anointing on the Holy Land. People feel like the Bible comes alive when they visit there because for the first time, they allow their imaginations to "see" what they've only read about. Seeing with your eyes what you've only read about helps your imagination to see more clearly. That's why visiting the Holy Land is so special.

Have you ever tried to assemble something using only the words in an instruction manual? You may read "Attach side A to side B using the F and G pegs," but you probably have to look at the included diagram to figure out what the instructions are talking about. This is why people say that a picture is worth a thousand words and why builders use blueprints. When we were building the Charis campus in Woodland Park, I remember sitting down with the architects and explaining to them what I wanted to see. But when they drew it out, it wasn't what I pictured. "No," I'd say, "I don't want that. I want this." And they'd go back to the drawing board. It took some time, but we just kept working at it until we could all see the same thing.

A builder would never attempt to construct a house by verbally explaining its layout to his tradespeople. If that were the only method he used to describe the design and function of a house, the homeowner might end up with an electrical outlet inside their bathtub!

But in a sense, that's what we do with the Word of God.

One of the main reasons people don't see the Word work in their lives is because they just read it. You can't *just* read the Word and expect it to produce change. You have to allow that Word to quicken your imagination until you "see" what you're reading. Even if you spend hours every week reading the Bible or quoting healing Scriptures, you won't see the fullness of those words come to pass in your life until you imagine yourself healed. You'd actually be better off reading one verse on healing and letting the truth within it paint a picture of who you are than reading five chapters in your "Read the Bible in a Year" plan and not even remember what book of the Bible you read. If you took the time to use your imagination to see yourself through the eyes of your covenant with God, as David did, you could slay giants too!

Chapter 5

NOT JUST THEORY

We should be experiencing life at a different level than our unsaved neighbors. In John 14:12, Jesus said, *"Verily, verily, I say unto you, He that believeth on me, the works that I do shall he do also."* "Verily" is an Old English way of saying "truly." Of course, everything Jesus said was true, and He never wasted words. So, anytime Jesus said "Truly, truly," He did so on purpose. He wanted to make it abundantly clear that He meant what He said.

> *Verily, verily, I say unto you, He that believeth on me, the works that I do shall he do also; and greater works than these shall he do; because I go unto my Father.*
>
> **John 14:12**

When I first began meditating on this Scripture, I went through each of Jesus's miracles, saying, "Lord, You said I could do the same works You did. You healed the sick. So, I'm going to heal the sick." I began imagining myself touching blind Bartimaeus, encountering the ten lepers, and healing the woman with the issue of blood, just like Jesus did. Then I got to raising the dead, and my imagination stuttered.

Again I said, "Lord, You said I could do the same works You did. You raised the dead. So, I'm going to raise the dead." I studied every biblical instance of someone being raised from the dead, and I began to imagine. I wrote the stories down. I rehearsed them in my mind. But instead of just seeing Jesus raise Lazarus from the dead, I personalized it. I saw myself raising Lazarus. I saw myself standing in front of the tomb yelling, "Lazarus, come forth!"

You may think I'm crazy, but before long, I started dreaming about raising people from the dead. Every night I'd raise twenty to thirty people back to life. It became so commonplace, it was hard for me to tell when I was awake and when I was asleep. Then one day—while I was definitely awake—a man died in one of my meetings. Without thinking too much about it, I commanded that man back to life and saw him raised from the dead. Jesus's words had become a part of me, and that man came back to life.

Proper use of the imagination should be something every believer cultivates. Yet I would say the majority of the people reading this book have never studied the imagination. You just haven't thought about it. Maybe it feels a little strange, a little childish. But Jesus said, *"Whosoever shall not receive the kingdom of God as a little child, he shall not enter therein"* (Mark 10:15).

Everyone uses their imagination. But sadly, by default, most people use it for negative things instead of positive ones. For example, if you suffer with depression, you are simply not controlling your imagination. Your thoughts are producing images of failure that say, *I'll never measure up. Things will never change. It's useless to try.* And though you may know those things aren't true, your emotions are firmly buckled into the driver's seat of your life and they *feel* true.

In 1 Kings 19, Elijah was in the same place. He had just called fire down from heaven, killed 850 false prophets, announced the end of a three-year drought, and outrun a chariot (1 Kgs. 18). (I think I'd call that a successful day!) But when Jezebel heard of his exploits and threatened to kill him (1 Kgs. 19:1-2), Elijah crumbled. Terrified, he ran for the desert:

*And when he saw **that**, he arose, and went for his life.*

1 Kings 19:3, emphasis added

Elijah fled when he saw *"that."* What did he see? The previous verse gives us some insight:

Then Jezebel sent a messenger unto Elijah, saying, So let the gods do to me, and more also, if I make not thy life as the life of one of them by tomorrow about this time.

1 Kings 19:2

Elijah saw himself dead, as Jezebel described, and he fled for his life. The way we see ourselves on the inside dictates our responses.

> *But he himself went a day's journey into the wilderness, and came and sat down under a juniper tree: and he requested for himself that he might die; and said, It is enough; now, O LORD, take away my life; for I am not better than my fathers.*
>
> **1 Kings 19:4**

> *And he came thither unto a cave, and lodged there; and, behold, the word of the LORD came to him, and he said unto him, What doest thou here, Elijah? And he said, I have been very jealous for the LORD God of hosts: for the children of Israel have forsaken thy covenant, thrown down thine altars, and slain thy prophets with the sword; and I, even I only, am left; and they seek my life, to take it away.*
>
> **1 Kings 19:9-10**

Elijah's imagination was out of control. He had just executed 850 false prophets of Baal, which I'm sure was a gruesome sight. He could probably still hear their cries and smell their blood. When Jezebel threatened to do the same to him, I suppose it was easy for Elijah's imagination to transpose his own face onto one of the bodies he'd just seen (1 Kgs. 19:2).

But instead of taking that thought captive (2 Cor. 10:5), Elijah wallowed in it.

"I'm the only one left!" he cried when God asked what he was doing hiding out in the desert. Of course, Elijah knew that wasn't true. Obadiah had just told him about the one hundred prophets he'd hidden from Jezebel (1 Kgs. 18:13). But it didn't matter what Elijah knew; he *felt* alone. Those feelings drove his words and his decisions.

Maybe you've been there. Maybe you're there now. You know it's not the end of the world, but it *feels* like it. And instead of controlling your imagination, you are allowing your thoughts to kill your vision for the future.

Twelve years after that man was raised from the dead in my meeting, I began thinking, *It's been a while since I raised anyone from the dead. I'm going to do that again.* And just like before, I began meditating. I went back through Jesus's examples. I went through Peter's and Paul's. I began imagining myself raising people from the dead, and soon I started dreaming again. Then, without warning, Jamie and I got a call. Our son was dead.

As we prepared for the drive into town, Jamie and I experienced grief like any parent would. But instead of dwelling on our loss, we began praising God and thanking Him for His goodness. We remembered prophecies we'd received about our son years earlier, and faith rose within us. By the time we got to the hospital, our son had been dead for five hours. He was stripped naked, on a slab in the morgue, and had a toe tag on—when he sat up and began talking.

Since then, over forty people have been raised from the dead through our ministry. We constantly get reports of the miracles our Bible college students see on the mission field. People are saved. Blind eyes are opened. The deaf hear. Not too long ago, a team of students prayed for a man in Nicaragua. The paramedics had given up on him, but these students raised him from the dead. During that same year, a baby was raised from the dead in Ecuador with a different group of students. It was awesome!

Who wouldn't want to see these kinds of miracles? Who wouldn't want to see their son raised from the dead? Who wouldn't want to see a family member healed of cancer? When the whole world is hurting, broke, and scared, who wouldn't want to be healthy, prosperous, and at peace? Everyone wants that. I'm sure many even pray for it. But not many are willing to do what it takes to see the Word work like that.

Two students at our Bible college in Atlanta heard me teach about this, and they began to work on their imaginations. When one of their family members was diagnosed with an incurable disease and given only a few days to live, those two rose up, spoke the Word of God, and that family member was healed! Another woman fighting cancer grabbed hold of this teaching and within twenty-four hours was seeing it work in her life. She had been going through radiation and looked like a cue ball. She lost every stitch of hair. Twenty-four hours after we prayed, her hair had grown nearly half an inch!

Brothers and sisters, there is a direct relationship between how you use your imagination and what you can receive from

God. It's honestly not that hard to get your body healed. God created our bodies to heal. The hard part is getting your imagination to work properly.

If I spent my life trying to receive from God based on the way others saw me or that old internal picture of an introverted hick from Texas, I can guarantee that you would not be reading this book. I would never have written it. You would have never heard of me. But I've let the Word of God change the way I see myself. I've let it define what I can do. Now I'm seeing the abundant life that Jesus provided at work within me (John 10:10). I'm doing the *"greater works"* (John 14:12), but only since my imagination opened the door.

Chapter 6

YOUR SPIRITUAL WOMB

Your imagination is powerful. It's like your spiritual womb. Just as a woman cannot give birth without first conceiving in her womb, you cannot give birth to the plans and promises of God without first conceiving them in your imagination.

I shouldn't need to explain this, but a woman cannot conceive a child alone. There is no stork. A woman cannot conceive by standing next to a pregnant woman or by drinking out of her cup. She has to be intimate with a man—and I'm not talking about the sharing of toothbrushes. A seed must be planted. The same is true for any believer who wants to receive something from God. He or she must become intimate with the Word.

First Peter says that we are born again by the incorruptible seed of the Word of God (1 Pet. 1:23). God's Word is seed.

But for that seed to work, it must be planted. This is why many believers pray for healing or prosperity yet never receive it. They may believe that the Word is true, but they have not become intimate with the Word. Their spiritual wombs are barren.

Years ago, I heard a testimony of a minister's wife with terrible eyesight. She was legally blind, and her glasses were as thick as Coke bottles. Though she believed her husband's preaching about healing, she just wasn't able to see it in her own life. No matter how many people prayed for her, she never saw the results she desired. The woman began to despair of ever being able to see without her glasses.

One day a healing evangelist came to her church. Knowing he would ask to pray for her, she did everything she could to avoid him. Finally, at the end of the week, the evangelist cornered her. "I want to pray for you," he said. "Take off your glasses."

The man prayed and then asked, "Can you see?" When the minister's wife began to open her eyes, the evangelist said, "Shut your eyes!" So, she shut her eyes.

He asked again, "Can you see?" Again, the woman began to open her eyes, but the healing evangelist rebuked her. "Shut your eyes!" he said. By now, the woman was beginning to wonder if the man was insane. How could she tell if her eyes were healed if she didn't open them?

A third time the man asked, "Can you see?" But this time when the woman began to open her eyes, he said, "I didn't tell you to open your eyes. You've got to see yourself seeing before you can see." Finally understanding what the man was trying to tell her, the minister's wife kept her eyes closed and prayed in the Spirit.

"I can see it," she said after a few minutes. "I can see myself seeing."

"Open your eyes," he said.

The minister's wife slowly opened her eyes. She could see!

If more of us understood this concept, we would get different results when we prayed. Instead, after we pray, we immediately open our eyes, check our wallets, and feel our bodies to see if something has happened. But miracles don't come from the outside; they come from the inside.

You cannot pray for healing while planning your funeral. You have to use your imagination to "see" the Word at work in your life. Don't wait for a physical manifestation to verify that God's promises are true. Instead, see yourself walking without pain. See yourself sleeping through the night, living instead of dying, eating what you haven't been able to eat.

During one economic downturn, when stock prices were plummeting, Jamie and I prospered. Our personal investments went up 50 percent. The only thing I can attribute that to is our obedience to the Holy Spirit and the internal picture we spent years cultivating from God's Word. Deuteronomy 28:8 says, *"The Lord shall command the blessing upon thee in thy storehouses, and in all that thou settest thine hand unto."* Jamie and I believed that. Even when we were so poor that we couldn't pay attention, we believed. We imagined what it would be like to go to the grocery store and walk out with everything we wanted. We imagined what it would be like to drive nice cars and to live debt-free. We didn't limit our imaginations to what our families or neighbors had experienced. We let God's Word show us a new picture.

The Hebrew word *yetser* was translated "imagination" or "imaginations" a number of times in the Old Testament. *Yetser* means "a form" or "conception" (*Strong's Concordance*). Your imagination is where you conceive. It is your spiritual womb. And just like a woman can't have a natural birth without natural conception, you can't have a spiritual birth without spiritual conception. In other words, before you can give birth to a miracle or to any of the promises of God, you must first conceive the Word in your imagination.

A familiar passage of Scripture, Isaiah 26:3, says,

> *Thou wilt keep him in perfect peace, whose mind is stayed on thee: because he trusteth in thee.*

The Hebrew word translated *"mind"* here is that same Hebrew word *yetser*. The imagination, which is part of the mind, is the spiritual womb where we conceive.

Proverbs 29:18 says, *"Where there is no vision, the people perish."* Remember, vision is the mental image formed in the imagination. What you imagine—what you see yourself doing, who you see yourself being—is what you will live out. Do you recall what the Lord said when He saw the people building the tower of Babel? *"Behold, the people is one, and they have all one language; and this they begin to do: and now nothing will be restrained from them, which they have imagined to do"* (Gen. 11:6).

Imagination comes *before* manifestation. If you can't imagine yourself doing what God called you to do or experiencing His promises, you'll never see those things come to pass with your physical eyes. You have to see them on the inside before you can see them on the outside.

Today's lifestyle is not conducive to what I'm talking about. We're just too busy. We mistakenly think that busyness is the same as productivity. But living life busier than a one-armed paper hanger is not good. Scripture says we need to take time to *"be still"* (Ps. 46:10).

I've never regretted taking time to set things aside, use my imagination, and seek the Lord. I always come back from that kind of downtime refreshed and carrying increased and clearer vision. It makes me wonder why I don't take more time off! It's easy to become so busy that we don't leave time to sit and use our imaginations purposefully. But without purposeful guidance and direction, our imaginations will begin to work against us.

The first time the word *imagination* is used in the Bible is in Genesis. After Adam and Eve fell and the people degenerated to the point that everything inside them was evil, their wickedness became so great that God grieved He had made mankind.

> *And GOD saw that the wickedness of man was great in the earth, and that every imagination of the thoughts of his heart was only evil continually.*
>
> **Genesis 6:5**

What a terrible commentary! The whole human race had drifted so far from God's intention that their imagination was *"only evil continually."* An unrenewed mind—an undirected imagination—gravitates toward evil, toward the negative. Psalm 140:2 says that those who don't know God *"imagine mischiefs in their heart."*

Whether or not you realize it, all wickedness, all sin, is conceived in a person's imagination. You can't go anywhere in your body that you haven't already been in your imagination. You cannot steal or commit adultery without first entertaining the idea in your mind. You may not be planning to rob the local bank or considering which coworker is most open to an affair, but you watch movies and television shows that portray people doing those things. They cheat, lie, and steal. They shack up with each other. They have affairs and live in homosexuality. They do things completely contrary to the Word of God. You may think it doesn't affect you, but according to 1 Corinthians 15:33, you're deceived: *"Evil communications corrupt good manners."* You cannot use the ungodliness of the world as entertainment without it affecting you. It's like digging a tunnel: You can't build a road or install a culvert through dirt and rock. You have to hollow out space for it.

Years ago in Colorado, the legalization of recreational marijuana appeared on the ballot. It was presented to the people as a "harmless" drug and a good way to raise tax revenue. Voters approved it in 2012, and now the state is bringing in millions of extra dollars of tax revenue every year. But it hasn't been the economic miracle advocates claimed. Homelessness has increased. Law enforcement needs have increased. Mental health issues have increased. But still, news broadcasters promote it as positive. They don't talk about the increased drug use in teens. They don't talk about the numbers of kids being treated in ERs because of the drug or the number of calls to Poison Control. They don't present anything negative about it. Their biased portrayal paints a picture that influences the way people think about marijuana.

Words are powerful. They paint pictures. They plant seeds. Every word you read, every word you speak, and every word you hear paints a picture in your mind. Proverbs 18:21 says, *"Death and life are in the power of the tongue: and they that love it shall eat the fruit thereof."* Watching ungodliness portrayed as normal or listening to the media present only half a story hollows out space in your mind. It gives your body permission to go there. And if you're not careful, that permission will bear fruit, and you will conceive sin (James 1:15).

Chapter 7

OVERCOMING TEMPTATION

Hebrews 11, the "Faith Hall of Fame," speaks of Abraham's obedience to go to a place he would later inherit, even though, at the time, he did not know where he was going. Hebrews 11:13 says he *"died in faith, not having received the promises, but having seen them afar off."* Abraham never inherited the Promised Land. Though God said He would give Abraham's descendants the length and breadth of it (Gen. 13:17), the only piece of land Abraham owned in Canaan was a small field with a cave where he buried his wife Sarah. He did not see the full manifestation of God's promise in his life; he only saw it *"afar off."*

Abraham's imagination saw all of God's promises come to pass before his hands could hold them. And every day he rehearsed those promises when he looked at the sky or walked across the land. Every day he remembered them as he did business and led his family. When the Lord changed Abraham's name from Abram (which means "high father" [*Strong's Concordance*]) to Abraham (which means "father of a multitude" [*Strong's Concordance*]), it was a reminder of God's promise (Gen. 17:5). It was a way out of the temptation to doubt. For twenty-six years, Abraham went around calling himself the "father of a multitude" before he had even one son!

God gave Abraham another reminder of His promise when He told Abraham to count the stars in the sky (Gen. 15:5) and the sand on the seashore (Heb. 11:12). Abraham lived in a tent, not a house. He didn't have artificial light. Abraham wore sandals, not boots. He lived in the desert. Every night as Abraham sat outside, he saw multitudes of stars. Every day as he walked the land, sand stuck in his toes. Every day Abraham remembered God's words. They engaged his imagination and developed a picture of who he was. That vision kept Abraham going by faith.

Each of us also has a picture of our life, but in many cases, it is a negative picture. What we see with our physical eyes is more real to us than what we see with the eyes of faith. We may have a word from God, but we don't nurture that word in our imagination. We don't conceive it.

Most people don't see the fullness of God's will come to pass in their lives because they expose themselves to *"evil communications"* (1 Cor. 15:33). They expose themselves to doubt and unbelief and exchange God's standard for the world's. They miss the mark.

There hath no temptation taken you but such as is common to man: but God is faithful, who will not suffer you to be tempted above that ye are able; but will with the temptation also make a way to escape, that ye may be able to bear it.

1 Corinthians 10:13

You cannot be tempted by something you don't think. I've been told that the first time people drink beer or liquor they don't like it, but because of a desire to be accepted by their peers, they persist, until they develop a taste for it. The same thing is true of smoking cigarettes. The first time a person smokes, they turn green and nearly get sick. The truth is, it's not the alcohol or the cigarettes that tempt a person. It's the desire to be accepted and to be like everyone else. And while God always provides a way out of temptation (1 Cor. 10:13), the best way to overcome sin and temptation is to not be tempted.

Many people think that is impossible, but it's not.

It is possible to become so focused on the things of God that all you think about is the Word and all you picture is His will. Just like Abraham, you can get so focused on God's direction that you become immune to temptation. Hebrews says:

These all died in faith, not having received the promises, but having seen them afar off, and were persuaded of them, and embraced them, and confessed that they were strangers and pilgrims on the earth. For they that say such things declare plainly

> *that they seek a country. And truly, if they had been **mindful** of that country from whence they came out, they might have had opportunity to have returned.*

Hebrews 11:13-15, emphasis added

The author of Hebrews went on to say that Abraham wasn't seeking a physical country. He was seeking a heavenly one (Heb. 11:16). But notice what the author said in Hebrews 11:15: *"And truly, if they had been mindful of that country from whence they came out, they might have had opportunity to have returned."*

Abraham and Sarah came out of Ur of the Chaldees (Gen. 11:31). Do you know who lived in Ur? Abraham's father and grandfather. Noah and his son Shem. All of the generations from Noah were still alive, but God told Abraham to leave them (Gen. 12:1).

The Bible doesn't make it clear, but Abraham was likely between thirty-five and forty when God first spoke to him. He was seventy-five when he finally left for Canaan (Gen. 12:4). It took him thirty-five years to obey God! But Abraham didn't obey 100 percent. He brought his nephew Lot with him.

God told Abraham to leave his father's house and *all* his kindred (Gen. 12:1). But since his brother had died, Abraham decided to bring Lot with him. He probably felt sorry for his nephew and wanted to care for him. While most people would consider that a noble thing, it was not a good reason to disobey God. (There is never a good reason to disobey God!)

God knew about Lot. He understood that Lot's father had died. But He also understood what would happen if Abraham brought Lot along. In case you don't remember, strife rose up between Abraham's and Lot's servants, and Abraham and Lot parted company (Gen. 13). Lot went to the fertile valley of Sodom. There, his whole family was taken captive, at least two of his daughters were destroyed when the Lord judged the city, all his belongings were lost, his wife was turned into a pillar of salt, and his other two daughters got him drunk and committed incest with him so they could have children! How could it have been worse for Lot if Abraham had obeyed God and left him behind?

Most Christians obey the same way. They get a word from the Lord and interpret it by what they think is best. They add to it or take away from it, thinking, *Surely God didn't realize* . . . People come to me all the time and say, "God told me to come to Charis Bible College, but I'm only ten years away from retirement. I can't leave that." So, they figure that God must have intended for them to come to Charis in ten years or that He should have waited ten years to tell them to come. No way! Don't try to figure out what God told you to do. Just do it.

Trust in the LORD with all thine heart; and lean not unto thine own understanding. In all thy ways acknowledge him, and he shall direct thy paths. Be not wise in thine own eyes.

Proverbs 3:5-7a

One of my employees worked for the California Highway Patrol before moving to Colorado. When he came to Charis, he was only two years away from retirement. People thought he was crazy to walk away from his pension and move his family across the mountains. But this man knew what God said, and he chose to obey. And it's been a good thing for his family. I don't know what would've happened if he hadn't obeyed, but there could have been tragedy. He could have been shot. His children could have been swept away by the culture. Who knows? The point is, you don't have to know. Just obey God and let the chips fall where they may. Don't lean to your own understanding or be wise in your own eyes.

A friend of mine, Rick Renner, was ministering in the Chicago area at a convention. He was not the speaker on the night in question, but he had planned to go to the meeting. However, as the day wore on, he had an increasing witness of the Spirit not to go that evening. He mentioned it to his wife, Denise, but they both thought it wouldn't be right to attend only the meetings Rick was speaking at. So, they decided to go anyway.

They made it all the way to the church, but finally, Rick was so convinced he should not be there that he turned around and went back to his hotel room. When he got there, the room had been broken into and his computer, which contained two books he was working on, was gone. Then he understood why the Lord was telling him not to go to the meeting that night.

Do you know what would have happened if Rick had stayed in the room? Nothing! Someone would have knocked on the door, but when they found him there, absolutely nothing would have happened. Likewise, if we obey the leading of the Lord, we might not know this side of glory what would have happened if we hadn't. But just like with Abraham and Lot, it is always better to simply obey God and leave the results with Him.

Just trust God. Abraham did. If Abraham and Sarah had been thinking of all they left behind, of all the people they would never see again, they would have been tempted to give up on God's promise and return to Ur. For them, returning was sin. Hebrews 11:15 says, *"And truly, if they had been mindful of that country from whence they came out, they might have had opportunity to have returned."* Since Abraham and Sarah weren't thinking of all they left behind, Hebrews says they weren't even tempted to go back. Man, that's awesome!

You may be thinking, *We could all be great men and women of God if we were never tempted to do anything else.* But you must understand that God did not give Abraham and Sarah anything He hasn't also given you (Heb. 8:6). If God will do it for them, He will do it for you. He does not show favoritism (Rom. 2:11). He has given you everything you need for experiencing an abundant life (2 Pet. 1:3 and John 10:10). He has given you His Word, His grace, and the Holy Spirit. And He has given you an imagination where the seed of His Word can be planted and produce life. Keep your imagination focused. Keep it directed on God's promises, and you will avoid temptation.

Chapter 8

LIVING ABOVE
THE NORM

Most Christians live life no differently than their unsaved neighbors. They let what they watch and read conceive sin in their imaginations. Instead of allowing themselves to imagine God's Word, they live vicariously through the characters they see in the movies. They get sick when their neighbors get sick. They fear what their neighbors fear. They lie as often, they gossip as often, and they get angry as often as their neighbors. Most Christians relate more to the world than they do to the things of God. They go to churches so dead that if someone dialed 911, half the church would be taken out before EMS found the right body. If someone raised their hand in worship, a pew neighbor would lean over to whisper, "It's down the hall, first door on the left." They think it's prideful to envision themselves laying hands on the sick (Mark 16:18) or living in prosperity and health (3 John 2).

Brothers and sisters, surrounding yourself with death will produce death in your life. *"Evil communications corrupt good manners"* (1 Cor. 15:33). It will chip away at your sensitivity to God's Word. Quit thinking on ungodliness. Quit imagining failure. Quit watching people struggle and die, thinking to yourself, *It's just normal.* For a Christian, it is not normal!

You are different from your neighbors. God created you to walk in victory (1 John 5:4). He qualified you to share in Christ's inheritance (Col. 1:12). Your life should be different. Surround yourself with people who believe and speak God's Word. Imagine the Word working in your life. Cultivate an atmosphere of faith. Then when the doctor says you are going to die, you will see a different picture. The Word will rise up inside of you, and you'll say, *"I shall not die, but live, and declare the works of the LORD"* (Ps. 118:17).

When the attacks on 9/11 happened, Christians everywhere were afraid to fly. They reacted the exact same way the world reacted. But God has not given any of us a spirit of fear (2 Tim. 1:7).

> *God is our refuge and strength, a very present help in trouble. Therefore will not we fear, though the earth be removed, and though the mountains be carried into the midst of the sea; Though the waters thereof roar and be troubled, though the mountains shake with the swelling thereof.*
>
> **Psalm 46:1-3**

If you are focused on the Word of God, it won't matter what the world throws at you. It won't matter what circumstances you face. You will not fear.

> *No weapon that is formed against thee shall prosper; and every tongue that shall rise against thee in judgment thou shalt condemn.* **This is the heritage** *of the servants of the* LORD, *and their righteousness is of me, saith the* LORD.

Isaiah 54:17, emphasis added

Supernatural protection is part of your heritage. But this verse also says you have to condemn each word that rises against you, each word that flies in the face of what you believe. God won't do it for you. You resist the devil, and he will flee from you (James 4:7). You have to do it. Words have power. They can be weapons (Is. 54:17) or honeycomb (Prov. 16:24). Every word you hear and speak is either drawing you closer to God and helping His Word come alive in your imagination, or it is making you numb to His promptings and bringing forth death in your life.

I was raised in a Christian home. I was taught conservative, Christian values, and I believed that what the Bible said was true. Though I'm sure I'd heard about homosexuality, adultery, and prostitution, I never thought about it. I never looked at pornography. In 1968, right after my encounter with the Lord, my mother thought I'd lost my mind. She wanted my Baptist pastor to talk me out of everything that had just happened, so she sent me with a group of kids on a three-week mission trip to Bern, Switzerland, where he could straighten me out.

The first night of the trip, we stopped in New York City. This little country boy from the backwoods of Texas was overwhelmed! We traveled downtown to see the sights. We went to Broadway. We walked around until the early hours of the morning. I walked down alleys handing out tracts. I talked to gang members. I witnessed to everyone. I didn't know enough to be afraid.

I remember turning down Forty-Second Street and finding an entire wall of girls at Forty-Second and Broadway. I still had some tracts left, so I walked down that entire strip, handing one to each girl. (It never dawned on me what they were doing there at three o'clock in the morning.) As I started preaching, they began to scatter. Pretty soon a pimp came up to me and tried to sell me one of his girls. I couldn't figure out what he was talking about. I remember him walking away, shaking his head, and throwing his hands up in the air. He must have wondered what rock I crawled out from under. But you know, I was never once temped by his words. I didn't know enough to be tempted. I didn't understand what he was trying to do. I didn't have to pray, "Help me, Jesus!" That may seem abnormal to you, but it just proves that you can't be tempted with something you don't think on.

If you are struggling with temptation or failure, it's because you've already been there in your mind. You watch adultery in movies. You watch people lie on television. You let your emotions go places with your favorite characters that you would never physically go. You allow your imagination to conceive sin, and it could give birth at a moment's notice.

Years ago, I heard of a couple with a marriage ministry. Some people were against what they were doing and tried to set the husband up. Since this man often traveled alone, they hired a stripper to go to his hotel room and present herself to him. Although he didn't plan to sin, he gave in to the temptation. They had set up cameras and had caught the entire encounter on tape. Of course, when the news got out, it ruined his ministry and was very damaging to his wife. During his apology, he said, "I'm sorry. I didn't want to do it. I was set up. I just couldn't hold myself back." But just like Abraham, he couldn't have been tempted with what he hadn't thought about.

It's a lot easier to avoid conceiving sin and negativity in your life when you practice denying it in your imagination. I can guarantee you I'm incapable of committing adultery today. I don't care what position you put me in, you could not make me do that to Jamie. I love her. I love God. My heart is fixed; it is set on fulfilling His will. Now, if I quit seeking God, maybe in a year or two I could do anything that anybody else could do. But I can't do it today. I'm simply not thinking on those things. I'm living above the norm because I've learned to control my imagination.

Casting down imaginations, and every high thing that exalteth itself against the knowledge of God, and bringing into captivity every thought to the obedience of Christ.

2 Corinthians 10:5

To see your life change, don't pray, "God, get rid of this person. Fix the government. Give me a new job. Do this. Change that." Instead, change your imagination. If you can imagine it, you can do it, but it's impossible to do what you've never seen yourself doing.

As I said, I grew up with a strict, legalistic background. In my church, dancing was of the devil. Dancing sent people to hell. You did not pass "Go," and you did not collect $200. You went straight to hell. I remember once when I was about fourteen, a girl asked me over to her house on a Wednesday night. It was the first Wednesday night church service I'd ever missed in my life. When I got there, I discovered that her parents weren't home and that several other couples were there too. When the music started playing and everyone began dancing, I couldn't get out of that place fast enough! I felt so convicted. I called my brother, and he got me to church before the service was over. That is the closest I've ever come to dancing in my life.

I'm no longer against dancing. The Word even tells us to dance before the Lord (Ps. 149:3). There's nothing wrong with it. People danced in the Bible. Sometimes people dance in our services. Once a man named Andy Hudson began dancing at our Ministers' Conference. He was flipping and spinning on the floor and wanted me to join in, but I just couldn't.

Afterward, I was talking to him and he asked, "Why can't you dance? You're not that old."

"I've never danced in my life," I said. "I've never imagined myself dancing."

"That's the reason you can't do it," he replied. And it's true. I can't dance because I've never seen myself dancing.

Your imagination is a creative force. It is a gift from God. Anything you can imagine can be done. I remember when one of the *Star Trek* series came out. They had these replicators on the show that could create anything at the push of a button. People used to think this kind of stuff was just fantasy, but now scientists have actually created 3D printers. My son has one. He can take a picture of anything, and the computer will print it. I've seen wrenches printed that you can actually hold in your hand and turn things with. I heard they're actually printing things like livers and body parts from a person's own DNA, hoping that these body parts won't have the same rejection factor as a transplant from someone else. That was just a dream twenty or thirty years ago!

What you dream and imagine matters. If you put your imagination to work and start focusing on the Word, you can start to live above the norm.

Chapter 9

THE BATTLEGROUND

We need to picture success. We need to see things from God's perspective and recognize that Christ has made us overcomers (1 John 5:4-5). We are victors. We are blessed. We are prosperous. We have peace. We are full of wisdom. We are healed, healthy, and whole. But often the switch from carnal thinking (thinking based on physical circumstances or past experience) to spiritual thinking (thinking based on the Word) is a battle. It's a battle of the mind.

> *For though we walk in the flesh, we do not war after the flesh: (For the weapons of our warfare are not carnal, but mighty through God to the pulling down of strong holds;) Casting down imaginations, and every high thing that exalteth itself*

against the knowledge of God, and bringing into captivity every thought to the obedience of Christ.

2 Corinthians 10:3-5

Spiritual warfare is different from what much of the church has taught. It is not the cosmic battle of good versus evil (Jesus already won that fight). It's not demonic strongholds setting up camp over cities or fighting to keep your prayers from reaching the ears of God. For the believer, spiritual warfare is a battle for your faith—and it is waged right between your ears.

All New Testament Scripture about spiritual warfare focuses its attention on the mind and imagination. Now, I believe that demons exist and that angels are real, but the only way they control or influence someone's life is through the imagination. This passage in 2 Corinthians says that *the weapons of our warfare are not carnal, but mighty through God"* (2 Cor. 10:4). It goes on to say that these weapons aren't used to deal with demons; they're used for *"casting down imaginations"* and bringing every thought captive to the obedience of Christ.

One of our students from Nigeria lived what I'm talking about. When she first came to school, she introduced herself to me by saying that she was plagued with demonic oppression. She said that she grew up around voodoo and was dedicated to the devil as a child. She'd been sexually abused, and even though she was now born again and Spirit filled, she struggled with fear. She struggled to sleep at night. She would wake up with cut marks on her. She felt like she was in a constant fight against demons.

"I believe you are struggling with a demonic attack," I told her, "but there's a reason they have access to you. The Bible says that Satan goes about as a roaring lion, '*seeking whom he may devour*' [1 Pet. 5:8]. He can't devour everyone."

I understand this usually doesn't bless people, but it is the truth. Christ stripped Satan of power (Col. 2:15). He can no longer wreak havoc in your life unless you forfeit your power to him—unless you give him place. It may not be intentional. It may even be through ignorance. But he cannot devour you without your consent and cooperation.

I continued telling this woman, "You're acting like the devil is the powerful force. Sure, he exists, but greater is He who is in you than he who is in the world [1 John 4:4]. Satan couldn't be doing these things to you if he didn't have something in you cooperating with him."

Like many people, she was not blessed by what I said, but she kept coming to me. We spoke several times during her first year at school. I told her, "You were raised in a culture where the devil is portrayed as this huge thing. You fear him. You honor his power. That's what's empowering him to do these things in your life."

Then one day she came to me, beaming, "I'm free!"

She told me she'd been completely delivered. She wasn't afraid. She was sleeping at night with no attacks. "I didn't know who I was in Christ," she said. "I didn't know my authority. And my ignorance was allowing Satan to do those things to me."

Brothers and sisters, if you're struggling with fear and oppression, if you've got demonic problems, stop cooperating with the devil! Renew your mind. Use your imagination to see who you truly are. Keep your mind stayed upon the Lord. I guarantee you, Satan will flee.

My grandmother lived with us until I was about seven years old. To accommodate her, my brother and I shared a room. When she died, my brother and I were so glad to get out of sharing a bedroom that I moved into my grandmother's old room almost immediately. But I only stayed there a few days. Toward the end of her life, my grandmother lost her mind and began dealing with demonic stuff. At night, while I tried to sleep in her room, her picture would come alive and travel all around that room. I never told anybody about it, because we weren't supposed to believe in those things. But it didn't take long for me to move back in with my brother. My brother didn't want to share a room, so he decided to try Grandma's old room. Two nights later, he was back. He never said a word.

For twenty years we kept the door to that room closed. Nobody went in there. We didn't heat it or keep it air-conditioned. It stayed separate. When my niece was only six months old, she'd scream just going near that room. She could be sound asleep, but if you took her into that room, she'd wake up screaming. You could walk back out, and she'd go back to sleep. Everyone knew something was wrong with that room, but nobody knew what to do about it.

When I discovered (contrary to what'd I'd been taught) that demons *did* exist and a lot of sickness and mental illness was demonic, I became so conscious of the devil that I started seeing a devil on every doorknob. I even began experiencing demonic manifestations. Demons would physically attack me. I remember being choked and thrown to the floor. I would bleed when no physical person was fighting me. It was demons inflicting those injuries. Even though I was rebuking and resisting, because I hadn't received balanced teaching on the subject, it was a struggle. Satan was whupping up on me—until the day I decided to do something about Grandma's old room.

Trembling, I opened the door and walked in. All the hair on the back of my neck stood on end, but I pled the Blood. I prayed in tongues. I rebuked. I resisted. I quoted Scripture and pled the Blood some more. I thought, *Oh God, I'm so glad I can't see these demons. If I could see their huge claws and ugly hides, I'd lose all faith. Thank You for protecting me.*

Then the Lord spoke to me. "You've got it all wrong," He said. "If you could see into the spiritual realm, you'd see that these demons are afraid of you. They're toothless, ant-sized creatures with big mouths. All they can do is bluff. They're hunkered down, trembling at *your* presence."

Instantly fear left me. I felt like the Incredible Hulk! I rebuked those demons in the name of Jesus, and they fled. It was over in minutes. Like our Bible student from Nigeria, I had been cooperating with the devil through fear. But as soon as I understood the truth—that the devil was defeated and I was victorious through Christ—I was set free (John 8:32).

That night was my weekly Bible study, and people went into that room to pray with others. Prior to that night, everyone avoided that room, although it was always available. They would use every other room in the house, but not Grandma's old room. Without me telling a soul what had happened that day, everything changed.

If the devil's beating up on you, you aren't keeping your mind stayed on the Lord. You aren't taking every thought captive and making it obey the Word. You aren't picturing who you are in Christ. Instead, you're letting your stinkin' thinkin' rob you. You're letting your imagination run wild, and you're conceiving sin, fear, and failure. Remember that what you conceive—unless there's an intervention—will be birthed (James 1:15). Don't allow your mind to dwell on such things. Keep your imagination under control, and win the spiritual battle for your faith.

Chapter 10

REMEMBRANCE

First Chronicles 28 gives an account of the end of David's life when he wanted to build a house for the Lord. Despite holding this dream close to his heart for much of his life, God overrode David's good intentions, saying, *"Thou shalt not build an house for my name, because thou hast been a man of war. . . . Solomon thy son, he shall build my house"* (1 Chr. 28:3 and 6). So, David passed the temple plans to Solomon. He didn't complain. He didn't accuse God of stealing his dream, nor did he try to undermine God's plans for Solomon. David was thankful for the part in Israel's history that God entrusted him to play, and he set about doing all he could to make Solomon's job easier.

That day, David gave the equivalent of billions and billions of dollars from the royal treasury (1 Chr. 22:14) for the building of the temple: *"gold for things to be made of gold, and the silver for things of silver,"* wood, precious stones, and marble

(1 Chr. 29:2). Then, in the presence of all the people, he gave a huge offering of his personal funds (1 Chr. 29:3-5). Following his example, the people also began to give, and David said:

> *But who am I, and what is my people, that we should be able to offer so willingly after this sort? for all things come of thee, and of thine own have we given thee. . . . O LORD God of Abraham, Isaac, and of Israel, our fathers, keep this for ever in the imagination of the thoughts of the heart of thy people, and prepare their heart unto thee.*
>
> **1 Chronicles 29:14 and 18**

To my knowledge, no other offering in history has come close to equaling what David and the people gave that day! Billions of dollars' worth of gold, jewelry, and family treasures came in spontaneously. David was so touched by the people's willingness to give that he prayed, "Lord, who are we that we could give like this? We were once slaves; we had nothing. Now look at this abundance! And to think that all this is just a portion of what You have already given to us!" He continued, "Lord keep this forever in the imagination of Your people. Help them remember this day. Don't let them forget."

David understood the importance of remembering and referred to it as keeping it in the imagination of the hearts of the people. As a matter of fact, earlier in his life, David wrote Psalm 103, which says:

*Bless the LORD, O my soul: and all that is within
me, bless his holy name. Bless the LORD, O my soul,
and **forget not all his benefits.***

Psalm 103:1-2, emphasis added

It is human tendency to forget. Just look at the children of
Israel. How often throughout their time in the wilderness did
the people forget what the Lord had done for them? It only
took three days for them to forget the Red Sea (Ex. 15:22-24).
Time and again they forgot the Lord's provision. "You have
brought us out here to kill us," they complained. "Let's go back
to Egypt" (Ex. 16:3 and 17:3). This is why the Lord gave the
Israelites laws commanding them not to remove their neighbor's landmark (Deut. 19:14) and to have annual feasts like the
Passover to commemorate special events and cause them to
rehearse all that God had done.

During one instance, shortly before Moses's death, Moses
gathered the people of Israel together for a few final instructions.
He appointed Joshua to lead the people into the Promised Land.
He reiterated the Law and recounted all the Lord had done for
them in the wilderness. He reminded the people how God had
delivered them from Egypt, destroyed the armies of their enemies in the Red Sea, and provided for them in the wilderness.
And the Lord told Moses to teach the people a song that would
"testify against them" when they rejected Him in the years to come:

*Now therefore write ye this song for you, and teach
it the children of Israel: put it in their mouths, that*

> *this song may be a witness for me against the chil-*
> *dren of Israel. For when I shall have brought them*
> *into the land which I sware unto their fathers, that*
> *floweth with milk and honey; and they shall have*
> *eaten and filled themselves, and waxen fat; then*
> *will they turn unto other gods, and serve them, and*
> *provoke me, and break my covenant. And it shall*
> *come to pass, when many evils and troubles are*
> *befallen them, that this song shall testify against*
> *them as a witness; for it shall not be forgotten out of*
> *the mouths of their seed: for I know their imagina-*
> *tion which they go about, even now, before I have*
> *brought them into the land which I sware.*

Deuteronomy 31:19-21

This amazes me. If I had the opportunity to help someone and drastically change their life circumstances—knowing they would reject and eventually come to despise my help—I don't think I would help them.

The Lord knew the Israelites would reject Him, and instead of turning away or writing them off, He told Moses to teach them a song, a song that would remind the people (and their children) of His goodness and testify against their unbelief.

Natural, human tendency is forgetfulness. If we don't purposefully keep our imaginations stayed on the goodness of God, we will forget what He has done in our lives, and our faith will suffer.

Not long ago, a couple approached me in near despair. They were facing a huge financial challenge and were praying for God to meet their need. But the deadline they'd set their faith upon was approaching, with no answer in sight. They didn't know what to do. But I knew this couple. I knew their story. I knew that God had saved their lives, delivering them from addiction and hunger. I knew He had pulled them off the streets and provided for them so abundantly that they were now providing for others. So, instead of praying for this couple as they requested, I spent a few minutes reminding them of all that God had already done in their lives. Before long, the two of them were weeping with joy. I did not meet their physical need. I did not give them a "Thus saith the Lord." Nothing in their circumstances changed. But they began remembering God's goodness, His faithfulness. It stirred their faith and they said, "If God can do that, He can take care of this!"

Memory is powerful. It engages our imaginations. But we must be intentional with it. We must use our imaginations to remember the things God has done for us, not the hurt of past circumstances. According to 1 Chronicles 29:18, we can't remember without engaging our imaginations.

Romans 1:21 talks about the link between thankfulness and the imagination:

> *Because that, when they knew God, they glorified him not as God, neither were thankful; but became vain in their imaginations, and their foolish heart was darkened.*

When we aren't thankful, when we don't remember what God has done or glorify Him as God, Paul says we become vain in our imaginations. Our hearts are hardened, and it becomes difficult to hear God's voice or see His work in our lives. To *glorify* basically means to put worth or value upon something or someone. If we're not glorifying God, then we are not esteeming or fully appreciating what He has done. Every day the sun comes up is a day to thank God. Every day He makes the earth turn and the seasons follow their courses. Every day His mercy and loving kindness follow us (Ps. 23:6). Every good thing we have and every breath we take—all of it comes from Him (James 1:17).

God has blessed us, but one of the signs of the end times is that people will become *"lovers of their own selves,"* proud, and **unthankful** (2 Tim. 3:2). That's one reason I have made international mission trips mandatory for Charis students. Sometimes it's important to step away from our culture (where we think being poor is not having five flat screen televisions, the newest car, and the fanciest phone) to recognize our many blessings. I once heard David Barton say that under certain circumstances, if a person makes less than $61,000 a year, they can qualify for government-issued benefits. Mercy! We don't understand what's going on in the rest of the world. I've heard that a person with no debt and ten dollars in their pocket has more money than the vast majority of the people on this planet. Ten dollars! We are blessed, blessed, blessed, and many of us don't even know it!

We take so many things for granted in America. Not valuing what God has done—that we're breathing, that we live in one of the most prosperous nations in the world, that God is moving and people are coming to know Him by the thousands—makes us ungrateful and blinds us to His goodness.

If we could take our grandparents or great-grandparents and translate them into today's lifestyle, they would be overwhelmed at our conveniences. We can travel halfway around the world in less than a day. We can put something in the microwave, push a button, and have a hot meal in two minutes. We can make phone calls without wires and get the latest news in minutes. Our great-grandparents would be shocked!

Do you realize how much more time we have now? Our great-grandparents spent the whole day just trying to survive. They grew their own food and made their own clothes. We have so much more free time than they did. The question is, what are we doing with that extra time? Are we glorifying God? Are we blessing others? Are we living out our true purpose?

When we take God's blessings for granted or aren't thankful, Romans says we become *"vain in* [our] *imaginations"* (Rom. 1:21, brackets added). That doesn't mean our imaginations cease to work. It means they just start working against us. We forget what God has done in our lives, and our imaginations begin gravitating toward the negative.

Chapter 11

CAN'T LOSE
FOR WINNING!

Peter urged us as believers to *"add to* [our] *faith virtue; and to virtue knowledge; And to knowledge temperance"* so that we would not become barren or unfruitful in life (2 Pet. 1:5-8, brackets added). Peter said, *"He that lacketh these things is blind, and cannot see afar off, and hath forgotten that he was purged from his old sins"* (2 Pet. 1:9).

Our ability to remember God's goodness is directly tied to the use of our imaginations. No one is as blind as the person who only sees what is staring them in the face, who has forgotten God's goodness. Scripture teaches that emotions follow thoughts. Emotions are a by-product of what the mind focuses on. If we aren't valuing what we have—if we're bemoaning all we don't have and are focusing on the negative, if we are fearful of what might happen—we are directing our imaginations to think on depressing things. And it will produce depression in our lives. Isaiah 26:3 says:

> *Thou wilt keep him in perfect peace, whose mind is stayed on thee: because he trusteth in thee.*

Peace is a by-product of what we think on. A person who fights depression is living with a vain imagination. The world may call it a "chemical imbalance" (and that may well be one of its symptoms), but their body is working exactly the way God designed.

If you keep your mind focused on God—on what is true, honest, just, pure, lovely, and of good report (Phil. 4:8)—you will have peace. If you don't feel peace, it's because you're thinking on the wrong things. Your emotions are following your thoughts.

Years ago, a woman came to me in tears. Her goal in life was to become a mother, but she and her husband had struggled to get pregnant. Finally, after months of trying, they discovered they were going to have a baby! However, during her most recent doctor's appointment, they were told she had a tubular pregnancy. In order to save her life, the doctor advised an operation to remove all her female organs. "But even if we do this," she said, "the doctor said there's only a 50 percent chance I'll survive."

Trying to come to terms with the imminent loss of her baby and any hopes for children, this woman came for prayer. "That's no big deal," I said to her.

Immediately the woman stopped crying and looked at me with eyes as big as dinner plates. You would have thought I slapped her. "You can do whatever you want," I continued. "You can go the doctor route. You can let them take out all your female parts. God loves you—and that won't ever change—but you'll never have natural children if you do that."

"What option do I have?" she sniffled. "If I don't do this, I could die."

"Believe God!" I exclaimed. "This is no big deal for God. It's not hard."

Long story short, the woman decided to believe God. She and her husband refused the doctor's treatment, signed page after page of legal documents absolving the doctor of liability, and set their faith to believe. Twenty-five years and many naturally born kids later, she is alive and well and declaring the works of God!

Brothers and sisters, these things are not difficult for God. Even cancer is no big deal. Cancer's not any harder to heal than a cold. You can't heal a cold, and you can't heal cancer. (Doctors can actually do more for cancer than they can for a cold. They can radiate it; they can cut it out. But they can't do anything for a cold. The medicines they give you to deal with the symptoms only dry out your sinuses, but they make the cold last longer.) The difference is the amount of fear associated with it. Catching a cold doesn't affect your imagination the same way developing cancer does. However, from God's standpoint, it's not any harder to heal cancer than it is to heal a cold.

Unfortunately, most people carry around a different image. Instead of remembering God's goodness and promises, they allow fear to direct their imaginations and control their emotions. It's been decades since I've been depressed or afraid. I simply don't allow myself to go there. I keep my mind stayed on the Lord.

> *Thou wilt keep him in perfect peace, whose mind is stayed on thee: because he trusteth in thee.*
>
> ### Isaiah 26:3

The Hebrew word translated *"mind"* in this verse is actually the word *yetser* and refers to the imagination. In the Old Testament, this word *yetser* was actually translated *"imagination"* four times (Gen. 6:5, 8:21; Deut. 31:21; and 1 Chr. 29:18) and *"imaginations"* once (1 Chr. 28:9). If you will keep your mind, specifically your imagination, stayed on God—if you will keep seeing yourself winning, keep seeing the promises of God coming to pass, keep thinking about what God has promised instead of what you see and feel in the natural realm—you will experience peace. You won't be anxious of sudden fear (Prov. 3:25). You won't know how to worry. You won't know how to disbelieve God. No matter what happens, your heart will be fixed.

Toward the end of Apostle Paul's life, he wrote to the church in Philippi, saying, *"For to me to live is Christ, and to die is gain"* (Phil. 1:21). By this time in Paul's life, he'd traveled much of the known world declaring the Gospel. His body was tired; it had been through a lot! He'd been threatened and beaten multiple times for his testimony. He'd endured prison, been shipwrecked, and known hunger, nakedness, and cold (2 Cor. 11:23-27). The fact that Paul was still alive was a testament to God's grace.

Paul wrote this letter to the church, knowing his time on earth was coming to an end. As he sat in prison again, he penned this struggle of longing for heaven yet knowing he was still needed on earth:

> *For I am in a strait betwixt two, having a desire to depart, and to be with Christ; which is far better: Nevertheless to abide in the flesh is more needful for you. And having this confidence, I know that I shall abide and continue with you all for your furtherance and joy of faith.*
>
> **Philippians 1:23-25**

Paul was not afraid to die. He knew this physical existence was a mere shadow of all there was to life, and he was looking forward to heaven. He even called dying *"gain"*; some translations say "great gain." But instead of going to be with the Lord, Paul chose what was most necessary: remaining *"in the flesh"* to help guide the new churches in right doctrine.

I understand his dilemma. I once received a book entitled *Intra Muros* by Rebecca Springer. It was originally published around the turn of the twentieth century and has since been published under different titles. In the book, Rebecca writes about her experience in heaven. She begins by saying (in my own words), "I'm not preaching. I'm not trying to make a new doctrine. I have no agenda but to share my experience and encourage others as I have been encouraged." At the time she wrote this book, nearly every family in the United States had lost someone in the Civil War. Many at the time thought life ended at death, and they struggled under the weight of their grief. But when Rebecca fell sick and died, she discovered that life doesn't just continue; it continues gloriously for all who believe!

When I received the book, I was traveling. I had no intention of reading it until I got home, but that night in my hotel room, I picked it up and couldn't put it down. I stayed up all night and read the entire book—and I had to preach the next morning! Then, shortly after I got home, I left Jamie with my suitcase and rushed off to a series of meetings. Later that day, I found her sitting on a chair in our living room completely awestruck. She had read the book. For the next month, the two of us had to use our faith to stay alive because we were so ready for heaven!

Brothers and sisters, you don't have to fall apart like a two-dollar suitcase every time the winds of circumstance blow in your life. This life is not all there is! If the doctor told me I was going to die, I wouldn't let it rock my world. Inside of me lies the same power that raised Christ from the dead (Rom. 8:11). If death couldn't hold Jesus in the grave, it doesn't have the power to put me there prematurely. But if worse came to worst and I didn't receive healing, I'd just go to heaven. I'd see Jesus face-to-face. I'd meet all my biblical heroes. I'd be reunited with my mom and dad, my sister—with all those who have gone before me. If the doctor told me I was going to die, it might be all I could do not to reach up and kiss him! For a believer, death is not the end; it's only the beginning (1 Cor. 15:54-55).

In the Christian life, you can't lose for winning. God is on your side. If you lose money, He has given you the power to get wealth (Deut. 8:18). You can make it back again. If you are fired unjustly, God is your source. He will provide your daily bread and will also provide for your reputation (Ps. 146:7). If you're sick, you can be healed. He is the Master Physician (Ex. 15:26). You can win in this life! But even if you die, you still win!

Chapter 12

AN ETERNAL PERSPECTIVE

Jesus never promised us a life without trouble. But He did promise that, through Him, we would overcome (John 16:33)! If you're not experiencing victory and you don't know peace, you don't have the right perspective. The *New Living Translation* of Isaiah 26:3 says, *"You will keep in perfect peace all who trust in you, all whose thoughts are fixed on you!"* If you're struggling with worry, depression, or stress, you're not keeping your imagination fixed on Him.

It doesn't matter what's happening at work. It doesn't matter what's going on in your body or bank account. It doesn't matter what society is doing. What matters is what's going on in your heart. I don't doubt that physical problems exist. I don't doubt that chemical imbalances exist. I know you can take a pill to affect your mood. But chemical imbalances don't cause depression. Depression causes chemical imbalances.

Regardless of what happens *to* you or *around* you, it's what you allow to dominate your heart—your imagination—that dictates how you feel and ultimately determines the course of your life.

> *Keep thy heart with all diligence; for out of it are the issues of life.*
>
> **Proverbs 4:23**

Jamie and I have been in situations that looked absolutely hopeless in the natural. I remember one instance that made worldwide news. Something that happened to us was mentioned on Paul Harvey's broadcast. He called us by name and said, "This is the worst thing I've ever heard." Yet in that moment, we had peace. We were hopeful.

Wendell Parr, a good friend who helped us start Charis, called me after hearing the news and said, "I know that you're bound to be struggling. Don't come in today. You can't minister right now."

"I'm coming in," I replied.

"But with what's happened to you . . ."

"Hey," I interrupted, "Jesus hasn't changed. I'm not telling those students about me. I'm telling them about Jesus. I'm coming in." And I ministered all day.

The only way to do something like that is to control your imagination and keep your eyes fixed on Jesus (Heb. 12:2).

> *While we look not at the things which are seen, but at the things which are not seen: for the things which are seen are temporal; but the things which are not seen are eternal.*
>
> **2 Corinthians 4:18**

This verse makes it abundantly clear that everything we can see with our eyes is temporary. Problems are temporary. Circumstances are temporary. Even relationships come and go. But unseen things—spiritual truths—are eternal. That's what Jamie and I focused on. That's what Apostle Paul focused on.

In his second letter to the Corinthians, Paul spoke of his suffering for the sake of the Gospel. He said that as ministers, he and the other apostles were *"troubled on every side, yet not distressed; . . . perplexed, but not in despair; Persecuted, but not forsaken; cast down, but not destroyed"* (2 Cor. 4:8-9). All of it was for the sake of those to whom they preached (2 Cor. 4:15). Paul went on to say:

> *For which cause we faint not; but though our outward man perish, yet the inward man is renewed day by day.*
>
> **2 Corinthians 4:16**

This verse applies to all of us, ministers and laypeople alike. No matter what is happening outside, our inward man can daily be renewed if we learn to control our thoughts.

As a society, we have become masters of excuses. We think, *Nobody knows the trouble I've seen; nobody knows my sorrow.* But no matter what your doctor said, it's not your hormones. It's not a chemical imbalance or a nutrient deficiency. No matter what the psychologist says, it's not "that time of the month" or the way you were raised. What you think on, you become. Convincing yourself that your problems are bigger or your challenges harder only distances you from the answer. You cannot be a victim and a victor at the same time.

You must let the Word of God paint a picture of success and victory in your life. Because in the light of eternity, what's happening to you is not that big of a deal.

You know, I've kept a journal since 1996. Sometimes I go back and read it to remember what God's brought me through. It helps me to be thankful. It also amazes me when I read some of the things that used to bother me. If I didn't have that journal, I would have totally forgotten them by now. They just weren't that important. But at the time, I thought they were a big deal.

For instance, I came home from a nightmare ministry trip a number of years ago. I won't go into the details, but after seventy-two hours of no sleep, my car broke down and I had to rent one to get home. The rental got stuck, so I had to borrow a car from a friend, and I put a scratch on the car! He got his whole car repainted at my expense.

I never wanted to deal with anything like that again, so I decided to buy two new cars (one for Jamie and one for me) that wouldn't break down. A week later, I backed my new car out of the garage and into the other new car. I wrecked both of them the first week!

As frustrating as that may seem, they were just cars. It didn't matter. No one was hurt. We got them fixed, and it was no big deal.

I'm telling you, Jesus is bigger than anything you or I could face in this life. But like Apostle Paul, we need to get the attitude that our current struggles are but a *"light affliction"* compared to the joy that awaits us in eternity.

> *For our light affliction, which is but for a moment, worketh for us a far more exceeding and eternal weight of glory; While we look not at the things which are seen, but at the things which are not seen: for the things which are seen are temporal; but the things which are not seen are eternal.*
>
> **2 Corinthians 4:17-18**

Paul could call his sufferings light because they were *"but for a moment."* And in those sufferings, he learned to look at the *"things which are not seen."* How do you look at things unseen? With your imagination. Paul said that everything seen is temporary.

Everything in the natural can be changed. Cancer can be changed. AIDS can be changed. Finances can be changed. Everything physical is subject to change and, according to Philippians, must bow its knee to that which is eternal, the name of Jesus (Phil. 2:9-10). This is so important. I understand that it is easier to preach than to live, but I'm telling you, it's worth the effort!

The Word of God is far superior to anything you can see with your physical eyes. It's worth the effort to meditate on the Word and let it paint a new picture in your mind. It's worth the effort to keep your imagination stayed on God, capturing any thought that exalts itself against the knowledge of Christ. No matter what's going on in your life, God has given you the ability to overcome. No excuses. No exceptions. You don't have to live under the circumstances.

Chapter 13

ACTIVE FAITH

Imagination is the frame your whole being is built upon. Just like the frame of a house or your body's skeleton, imagination gives structure. It dictates, in large part, your life's experiences. If you're not experiencing the abundant life Jesus died to provide, your imagination could be to blame. Psalm 103 says:

> *Like as a father pitieth his children, so the L*ORD *pitieth them that fear him. For he knoweth our frame; he remembereth that we are dust.*

Psalm 103:13-14

God knows what we are; He *"knoweth our frame."* Like the words *imagination* and *mind* (referred to previously), this word *"frame"* was also translated from the Hebrew word *yetser*. God knows our imaginations, yet He is merciful and understands us. He knows that our imaginations have the tendency to gravitate to evil, to the negative. And He made a way to change that. He became a man. He became dust like us. And through the new birth, we now have the ability to use our imaginations in a positive way.

Remember, imagination is the ability to see with your heart what you can't see with your eyes. And for a Christian, the ability to see what can't be seen—the ability to walk by faith—is a part of who we are. Or at least it should be. Second Corinthians 5:7 says, *"We walk by faith, not by sight."* Unfortunately, most Christians walk by sight instead of by faith.

A number of years ago, I was playing golf with some friends and got badly sunburned. A blister formed on my ear that just wouldn't heal. I got tired of it after a few months and ripped it off. The sore bled and oozed for six years. I don't know exactly what it was; I never went to a doctor or had it tested, but many people told me it was a melanoma cancer. Once while I was in Charlotte, North Carolina, I prayed for two people who'd dealt with the exact same thing and had actually had parts of their ears surgically removed. As I laid hands on them, I believed and spoke the Word over their situations while my own ear was oozing. As ironic as that seems, I wasn't bothered. I knew I was healed, and I knew my ear would have to line up with what I believed.

Everywhere I went, people asked me about that sore, and I would say, "I'm healed in the name of Jesus." I must have said it a thousand times in six years, and that healing did finally manifest.

My point, brothers and sisters, is that learning to walk by faith and use our imaginations properly is a process. I am in the middle of that process, just like you. Over the years, I've learned that God, like any good father, is much more interested in our progress than our results. For example, today in the ministry, I have to have thousands of dollars every hour just to pay my employees and meet our other obligations. That translates to millions of dollars per month! I can't supply enough money to operate the ministry for one week outside the grace of God, let alone fifty-two weeks a year! At one time, that type of pressure would have killed me, but I don't worry about it today. I don't lose sleep. That's what faith is.

Hebrews 11:1 says, *"Faith is the substance of things hoped for, the evidence of things not seen."* Faith isn't based on the physical reality of what we can see with our eyes, hear with our ears, or hold in our hands. There is more to this life than what our five senses can tell us.

As you're reading this book, television and radio signals are all around you. Wireless internet and phone signals are floating past too. You can't see them, but they're there. Television and radio stations don't start broadcasting signals when you turn on your set. They broadcast all the time. You simply need a device to help you tune in and perceive them. In the spiritual realm, faith is that device. Faith helps you perceive spiritual reality.

God is a Spirit (John 4:24), and we are created in His image as spirits (Gen. 1:26). God communes with us Spirit to spirit. My teaching *Spirit, Soul & Body* explains this principle better than I can here, but everything we receive from God comes first to our spirits. Our born-again spirits have no trouble receiving from or hearing the voice of God. But before our bodies can experience God's promises or hear His voice, we have to get our souls tuned in (Philem. 6).

Modern Christians spend a lot of time running around the country attending special services, hoping for a "word from God." We fast, trying to stir God's compassion. We wail, "Oh God, send revival! Save the lost! Stretch forth Your hand to heal! Move among us!" But God doesn't need to move. He's not the one who's stuck! He doesn't need to "stretch forth His hand." He did that 2,000 years ago!

We have the same power inside us that raised Jesus Christ from the dead (Rom. 8:11 and Eph. 1:18-20). The power of God is not out there somewhere. We don't have to find it or pray it down. We don't need to fight to get our prayers through the demonic realm. We don't have to get our prayers above the ceiling! God—the Creator of the universe—lives inside every born-again believer. That's why we bow our heads to pray. All we have to do is begin to recognize what we have (Philem. 6) and learn how to release it by faith.

Faith is our positive response to God's grace. It produces a confidence in Him that breeds action.

> *Even so faith, if it hath not works, is dead, being*
> *alone. Yea, a man may say, Thou hast faith, and I*
> *have works: shew me thy faith without thy works,*
> *and I will shew thee my faith by my works. . . .*

For as the body without the spirit is dead, so faith without works is dead also.

James 2:17-18 and 26

Faith without works is dead. To know that by Jesus's stripes you were healed (1 Pet. 2:24) and yet continue to worry or stress about what might happen as you walk out that truth is not faith. It's not faith until you see it with your heart and enter rest, confident in God's promise. You can get to the point where what you see with your heart—inspired by the Word of God and quickened by the Holy Spirit—is more real to you than what you see with your eyes or feel in your body.

Many people confuse faith with a belief system or the acknowledgment of a set of ideals, but faith is confidence in God (Ps. 27:13). While we were building The Auditorium for the Charis campus at The Sanctuary in Woodland Park, we ran out of money. We were committed to building the entire campus debt-free, so we stopped construction with the building only partially completed. Several of my staff members asked, "Are you discouraged, Andrew? Does this construction pause bother you?"

"No," I replied. "I'm not concerned. In my heart, I know it's done. I'm not sure about the timing. I don't know how much effort it will take to get there, but I see it done. I'm not going to worry about it." Less than three months later, we were back at it.

Several years prior, when we bought our ministry building on Elkton Drive in Colorado Springs, the building needed

$3.2 million in renovation to retrofit it for our needs. The Lord told me to do it debt-free, but at that time, with the income we were bringing in, it would've taken over a hundred years to save enough money to meet that need!

My employees encouraged me to take the need to my partners, but instead, I sat in that building for three or four months. I knew I would eventually need to contact my partners, but I first needed to strengthen my faith. I needed time to engage my imagination. I had our contractor put duct tape on the floor of the building, showing every wall and every door. I spent hundreds of hours walking those "halls." I'd walk around and pray. I'd imagine it full of students. I went through the "doors" thinking about what I wanted each room to look like, praying for the students who would come. In the auditorium, I put five-gallon buckets upside down with a piece of plywood over the top to create a "stage." With no one around, in total darkness, I would stand on that platform and preach. I walked those floors until I could see everything in my imagination. When I finally wrote down the vision and shared the need with our partners, they gave over and above anything the ministry had ever seen. In fourteen months, we had the $3.2 million needed to renovate that building!

In both those instances, I had to walk by faith. I had to take the things God showed me in the Word and meditate on them until I could see the solution in my imagination. Most Christians in similar situations panic. They stress over the problem or act on impulse. They don't wait. They don't consider the Word. They don't take time for their imaginations to conceive the answer. They don't walk by faith.

Brothers and sisters, we have everything we need to succeed! But just like we have to exercise a muscle to improve its performance, we have to exercise our faith. Imagination helps us do that.

Chapter 14

EXERCISING
YOUR FAITH

God has already given us everything we need to overcome (2 Pet. 1:3), but it takes faith to agree with God and trust that what He said will be accomplished. One of the ways we do that is through our voices. I have a reputation among Charis students for only speaking the Word, for only tolerating faith. Apparently, I correct students who spew doubt and unbelief; consequently, most have learned to speak a certain way around me. The problem is, they don't speak the same way when they're alone. Most of them would be embarrassed to speak to me the way they speak with their friends or think in their minds. But self-talk is where the battle is won or lost. It helps direct our imaginations.

Have you ever heard your voice on a recording? You hear yourself differently than other people hear you. Other people hear you with their outer ears only. You hear your voice with your outer and inner ears, and it has a different effect.

Your words affect you differently than they affect others—they are more important. When I first learned this truth, I would stand in front of my mirror, look at myself eyeball to eyeball, and say, "You are righteous." The first time I said that, all the hair on the back of my neck stood up! I thought, *Oh God, don't strike me dead. I'm just trying to say what the Bible says.* I had so many years of unworthiness rooted in me that it took a lot of effort to say those words. I had to force myself to do it.

I had to do the same thing when the Lord called me into the ministry. I had to convince myself that what God said about me was true. To do that, I needed to hear myself speaking God's Word. So, I would look in the mirror and say, "You will speak in front of thousands of people. You will go to the nations. You will do what God called you to do."

Jesus's statement in Mark 11 illustrates this concept. After Jesus cursed the fig tree, His disciples were shocked when they walked past and saw that it had withered from the roots and died. Jesus said to them, *"Have faith in God"* (Mark 11:22). Now, we don't have the benefit of hearing the inflection of His voice, but I believe Jesus was saying, "What's wrong with you guys? All you need is faith." He went on to say, "If you have even a little faith [some accounts say "faith as a grain of mustard seed"], you can say to this mountain . . ." Notice that Jesus didn't say "You can talk to God about the mountain." No, He told the disciples to talk to the mountain:

*For verily I say unto you, That whosoever shall say
unto this mountain, Be thou removed, and be thou
cast into the sea; and shall not doubt in his heart,
but shall believe that those things which he saith
shall come to pass; he shall have whatsoever he
saith. Therefore I say unto you, What things soever
ye desire, when ye pray, believe that ye receive
them, and ye shall have them.*

Mark 11:23-24

Something happens when you hear yourself speak the Word.
It almost becomes more important, more real. It helps to build
your faith. Romans 10:17 says, *"Faith cometh by hearing, and
hearing by the word of God."* Faith comes when you hear yourself (and others) speak God's Word.

Jesus said we were to speak to our mountains. But instead
of doing that, Christians often pray, "Oh God, I've got a problem. The doctor said . . ." or "My bank account says . . ." They
say things like "Oh God, do something! I can't do anything. I
am nothing; I have nothing, but You can do all things. God,
help me!"

You'll die praying like that. God's raising-from-the-dead
power lives in you (Eph. 1:18-19). Agree with Him! Speak to
your mountain. Say, "Sickness, in the name of Jesus, get out
of my body! Cancer, I curse you. In Jesus's name, dry up and
die in these cells." Use your tongue like a weapon. Curse what
Satan is trying to use to destroy you. Speak life to your body
according to Proverbs 18:21. Thank God for His grace, and see

His anointing flow through your body and make every cell well in Jesus's name.

In 2001, I met a precious Presbyterian lady who was very sick. For seven years she'd dealt with pain so severe, she was nearly an invalid. The only way she could cope was to cover herself in magnets. Somehow the magnetic field helped lessen her pain. She spent every day lying in bed, wrapped in a magnetic blanket.

When I met her, she said, "I know all things work together for good, so I know God has a purpose for my pain."

"That's not true," I said. "God has nothing to do with sickness. He's not the one making you sick. He doesn't control that." Like most Christians who first hear this truth, she was shocked.

"But I believe God can be glorified in all this. He'll get a testimony out of it eventually."

"The greatest testimony you can have in this," I replied, "is to get healed." And I began countering all her wrong thinking with the Word of God. I taught her about 1 Peter 2:24 and Mark 11:23. I told her that God had already provided healing for her body and given her the authority to combat Satan's schemes. She didn't need to beg God and keep asking Him to do what He told her to do. A bit later, I prayed for her and she was instantly pain-free! She took off her blanket, stood up, and started moving around.

"I don't have any pain!" she said. "I do have a little stinging in my lower back. Why do I have a stinging?"

"You didn't tell me you had a stinging," I said. "I didn't talk to stinging; I talked to pain." Then I spoke to the stinging and commanded it to leave. It did.

But just as this woman was preparing to leave, she froze and turned to me. "The stinging is back," she said.

"Well, I've been teaching you what to do," I replied. "*You* pray."

Now, you've got to remember that forty-five minutes prior, this woman was a Presbyterian. She prayed, "Father, I thank You that You did not give me this sickness. This is not Your will for me. It is Your will that I am healed. Your Word says that by Jesus's stripes I am healed. I claim my healing in Jesus's name." I think she prayed a pretty good prayer for a Presbyterian! She spoke the truth. She didn't blame God for her problems. But she still didn't pray the way God told us to pray.

"Do you still feel the stinging?" I asked.

"Yes. Why is the stinging still there?"

"Because you didn't do what God told you to do. He said to speak to the mountain. You talked to God. You told God what you believe, but you didn't take your authority and speak to the stinging."

"You mean I'm supposed to say 'Stinging, stop in Jesus's name'?" she asked.

"Yes."

"Okay, I will." And she prayed again. "Stinging, in the name of Jesus . . ." She stopped right there and said, "It's gone!"

I see this woman nearly every year when I travel to Charlotte, North Carolina, and she's been living a productive, pain-free life since 2001! She's told me that the symptoms have come back a couple of times, but each time, she takes her authority and they leave.

If you're struggling to respond to life's circumstances with faith, start checking your words. Are they true—not factual, but true—and based on God's Word? Are you saying things like "By His stripes I was healed" (1 Pet. 2:24); "I will lay hands on the sick and they will recover" (Mark 16:18); and "I am above only and not beneath; I am the head and not the tail" (Deut. 28:13)? Are you declaring "I have the mind of Christ" (1 Cor. 2:16) and "My children are taught of the Lord and great is their peace" (Is. 54:13)? You have to learn to speak to yourself in faith, because what you hear and speak on the inside will become your meditation.

Chapter 15

FIRST STEPS

Ephesians 4 says:

> *This I say therefore, and testify in the Lord, that*
> *ye henceforth walk not as other Gentiles walk, in*
> *the vanity of their mind, Having the understand-*
> *ing darkened, being alienated from the life of God*
> *through the ignorance that is in them, because of*
> *the blindness of their heart.*

Ephesians 4:17-18

These verses don't connect with a lot of people, but I once spent an entire year meditating on nothing but Ephesians 4. These verses in the middle of the chapter are profound. They explain that in light of the new life we've been given in Christ, we as believers must stop walking like Gentiles (or those who don't know the Lord) in *"the vanity of their mind."* The word *vanity* means "futility" (*American Heritage Dictionary*). Paul said we're not supposed to walk like someone who doesn't know the Lord and who isn't using their mind or imagination properly.

You know, sin isn't smart. Just look at some well-known ministers who had success reaching millions of people and yet continued to walk like Gentiles. They entertained prostitutes and embezzled ministry funds, thinking they wouldn't get caught or that it wouldn't matter since they weren't hurting anyone. They allowed their emotions and the lust of the flesh to destroy their ministries. They hurt their families. They hurt the church. They lost everything. If they'd been using their heads, they would've never jeopardized that.

Sin isn't smart. Yet people sin. They lie, cheat, and steal. They slander others. They get drunk and do drugs. They puke their guts out hanging over a dirty toilet. They damage their internal organs, lose their jobs, go broke, destroy their families, and make fools of themselves. Sin is stupid.

As Christians, we shouldn't live like a lost person who does whatever feels good in the moment without thinking about the consequences. There are consequences to sin. Romans 6:23 says, *"The wages of sin is death."* Sin will take you further than you want to go, keep you longer than you want to stay, and cost you more than you want to pay. You don't want to sin. You don't want to walk in the vanity of your mind.

One definition of the Greek word translated *"vanity"* in Ephesians 4 is "transientness" (*Strong's Concordance*). A transient is a homeless person, someone who wanders, who lives on the streets or sleeps under a bridge. When I was a kid, we called them bums. As believers, we shouldn't allow our minds to function like that. We shouldn't let them wander or be unproductive. We need to use our minds to weigh our words and actions and to focus on the prize of our high calling in Christ (Phil. 3:14). Proverbs says:

> *Let thine eyes look right on, and let thine eyelids look straight before thee. Ponder the path of thy feet, and let all thy ways be established. Turn not to the right hand nor to the left: remove thy foot from evil.*
>
> **Proverbs 4:25-27**

A focused eye—a focused imagination—is necessary for a prosperous and successful life. Without it, Ephesians says that our understanding becomes darkened and we alienate ourselves from the kind of life God has prepared for us in Christ.

> *This I say therefore, and testify in the Lord, that ye henceforth walk not as other Gentiles walk, in the vanity of their mind, Having the understanding darkened, being alienated from the life of God through the ignorance that is in them, because of the blindness of their heart.*
>
> **Ephesians 4:17-18**

The Greek word translated *"understanding"* here is *dianoia*. This Greek word literally means "deep thought" (*Strong's Concordance*). Not casual thought, not surface thought, but deep thought. We could compare it to meditation. This same word *dianoia* is found in Luke 1:51, where it is translated as *"imagination."* This verse says that God has *"scattered the proud in the imagination of their hearts."* You can't understand without imagination, and if your imagination isn't functioning properly, you won't understand properly. Your understanding will be darkened—you won't be able to "see"—and you will become *"alienated from the life of God."*

This is exactly what happened to the Israelites throughout the Old Testament and into Jesus's ministry. Jesus, quoting Isaiah, said:

> *And in them is fulfilled the prophecy of Esaias, which saith, By hearing ye shall hear, and shall not understand; and seeing ye shall see, and shall not perceive: For this people's heart is waxed gross, and their ears are dull of hearing, and their eyes they have closed.*

Matthew 13:14-15a

What a terrible state to be in! Unfortunately, this state describes many in our world today, even many who believe— maybe even some who are reading this book. People come to me all the time asking me to pray that God would speak to them and show them His will. Yet Jesus said that His sheep hear His voice and the voice of a stranger they would not follow (John 10:3-5). Jesus didn't say His sheep *could* hear His voice; He said they *do* hear His voice.

You don't need me to pray that God will speak to you and give you direction. God is speaking constantly. You just need to tune your ears to hear. Use your imagination to help you understand.

Jesus went on to say, in Matthew 13, that if the people would learn to hear and see properly, they would understand with their hearts and He could work in their lives (Matt. 13:15). He told His disciples:

> *Blessed are your eyes because they see, and your ears because they hear. For truly I tell you, many prophets and righteous men longed to see what you see but did not see it, and to hear what you hear but did not hear it.* **Consider***, then, the parable of the sower.*
>
> **Matthew 13:16-18,**
> *Berean Study Bible*, **emphasis added**

We have to take time to *"consider"* God's Word. We have to meditate on it until we understand, until it forms an image inside us. Psalm 1 says:

> *Blessed is the man that walketh not in the counsel of the ungodly, nor standeth in the way of sinners,*

> *nor sitteth in the seat of the scornful. But his delight*
> *is in the law of the LORD; and in his law doth he*
> *meditate day and night.*

Psalm 1:1-2

We need to meditate in the Word of God day and night. Meditation is part of the imagination. As a matter of fact, Psalm 2:1 asks, *"Why do the heathen rage, and the people imagine a vain thing?"* That word translated *"imagine"* is the same word translated *"meditate"* in Psalm 1! One of the ways we meditate is through our imaginations.

I'm always amazed at the number of believers—even Spirit-filled ones—who can quote the Bible yet never see it produce change in their lives, never experience its power. The only way you can continue to think and act the way you did before you got saved is to ignore this important principle of meditation.

Many people have more knowledge of the Word than they have experience in it. You need to do more than just read the Bible. You need to think about it and apply it. Put yourself in the character's place and ask, "What does this mean to my life?" Let what you read form an image in your imagination. Don't just see Daniel standing up for what's right in the midst of an oppressive government; see yourself in his shoes. Don't just see David defeating Goliath; see yourself defeating the giants in your life. Don't just see Jesus healing the sick; see yourself healing the sick. In John 14:12, Jesus said, *"The works that I do shall* [you] *do also; and greater works than these shall* [you] *do; because I go unto my Father"* (brackets added).

Have you seen anybody raised from the dead? Have you seen blind eyes opened? Have you witnessed the deaf hear or the lame walk? If not, then you still have some meditating to do.

Chapter 16

THE POWER OF HOPE

Aproperly directed imagination is the most important and most underutilized function of our lives—both physically and spiritually. Our whole lives are built around imagination. Physically, we can't function without an imagination. We can't read or remember or properly communicate without one. We can't relate to God without an imagination either. Our imaginations help us believe and dream about the future. And while this concept of the imagination is found throughout the Bible, it's not always called "imagination."

When Adam and Eve sinned, they subjected themselves and all of creation to the effects of sin. Praise God, Jesus liberated us from sin's eternal effects, but creation (and our bodies) still wait for liberation. Like a woman in childbirth, creation groans in eager expectation of the *manifestation of the sons of*

God" (Rom. 8:19). Romans 8 goes on to say that our spirits also groan. Even though we've been given the *"firstfruits of the Spirit"* (Rom. 8:23) as a deposit, we wait for our redemption to be completed at Christ's return, when we receive our new, glorified bodies that cannot be touched by sin or death (Rom. 8:23). And because we wait for something we cannot yet see, we *"hope"* for it:

> *For we are saved by hope: but hope that is seen is not hope: for what a man seeth, why doth he yet hope for? But if we hope for that we see not, then do we with patience wait for it.*
>
> **Romans 8:24-25**

Imagination is the ability to see with our hearts what we can't see with our eyes. Hope is its New Testament counterpart. When I first began studying imagination, it seemed that every Scripture I found used the word *imagination* in a negative way. The only positive use I could find was David's prayer in 1 Chronicles 29:18 where he asked God to help the people remember their generosity in giving. I couldn't understand why something that seemed so powerful and foundational to our faith should be treated so negatively. But as I meditated on these verses in Romans 8, it suddenly dawned on me—imagination and hope had the same definition! *Imagination* is the word the Bible uses to describe the unregenerate (and predominantly negative) imagination. *Hope* is the way New Testament writers refer to our positive imaginations.

Romans says we are *"saved by hope"* (Rom. 8:24). Hebrews talks about receiving from God based on our *"assurance of hope"* (Heb. 6:11-12) and how hope becomes an anchor for our souls (Heb. 6:19). Hope is seeing what can't be seen. It helps us focus on God. It keeps us centered and is like an anchor that steadies us when the winds of circumstance or the opinions of man blow. (You know, if you don't anchor a ship—if you just let it sit in the water—even without a motor or sail, the waves will carry it away. It'll drift off to who knows where. But an anchor keeps the ship steady.) Hope keeps us from living life like a yo-yo or a ship adrift. It keeps us from getting off course. Hope is a positive imagination.

People often put faith and love on a pedestal, but rarely do they esteem hope. I've even heard people blast those who say "I hope so" or "I'm hoping for . . ." People in the faith camp hit them with "Stop hoping and believe!" as if hope is something bad. But 1 Corinthians 13:13 lists hope among the three great virtues. Hope is important. It gives our faith something to work with.

> *Now faith is the substance of things hoped for, the evidence of things not seen.*
>
> **Hebrews 11:1**

Many people (myself included) use this verse to define faith. But notice what it says about hope: *"Now faith is the substance of things **hoped** for"* (emphasis added). Faith gives substance to what we hope for; it births the things we see in our imaginations. If we don't conceive something in hope, faith cannot birth it.

I was listening to Charles Capps teaching along these lines, and he told a story about a man who lived his whole life in the backwoods somewhere, rarely coming to town. The man in his story knew very little about modern conveniences, and one day he was exposed to air-conditioning for the first time.

At a town meeting, surrounded by townsfolk, this man and the place where they all gathered began to get hot. The man watched as an usher calmly walked over to the wall and turned a dial. Within seconds, the man started to feel cold air blowing. Amazed, he stopped listening to the message and considered the thing on the wall. As soon as the meeting was over, he approached the usher and asked, "How did you make the cold air start blowing? What is that thing?"

The usher said, "That's a thermostat."

"Can anybody get a thermostat?"

"Sure. Just head down to the hardware store."

On the way back to his cabin in the woods, the man stopped and bought a thermostat. He hung it on the wall as soon as he got home and immediately tried it out. But no air blew. The man waited for it to get hot and tried again. No cold air. He couldn't figure out what was wrong; he did exactly what he saw the usher do! Of course, the man didn't realize that the thermostat wasn't what produced the cold air he'd enjoyed during that meeting. It only activated the air conditioner's power unit—a power unit he didn't have.

You see, a thermostat is to an air conditioner what hope is to faith. Hope is not the power unit; it only activates the power unit. The difference between that man and you or me is that we *do* have a power unit—a power unit called faith (1 John 5:4). Galatians tells us that every born-again believer is equipped with *"the faith of the Son of God"* (Gal. 2:20). We all have faith. We just have to learn to activate it.

Once when Jamie and I were considering buying a new car, we decided to visit a dealership and look around. We weren't planning to buy anything that day; we just wanted to start the process in our own minds and ask a few questions. Shortly after we arrived, a salesman approached. I began asking him questions like "What kind of gas mileage does this car get?" "What's included in the base price?" and "What's covered in the warranty?"

He ignored my questions. Instead, he opened the door and said, "Get in."

"Oh, I'm not interested in buying today," I replied. "I just have a few questions."

"That's all right," he said. "Try it out."

When I sat in the front seat, he said, "You look good in there! Is it comfortable? You can adjust the seat electronically. Would you like to take it for a spin?" Then all the way around the block, he said things like "Don't you love that new car smell? . . . Doesn't it handle well? . . . What color do you like? . . . Can't you imagine driving this to work next week?"

That salesman knew what he was doing! I'm sure he'd never listened to my teaching on imagination, but he certainly understood imagination's power! When I got back into my car, it wasn't the same. I noticed every scratch, every piece of dust. I missed the new car smell—the same smell I knew I could buy in a can at Walmart for a couple of bucks. My imagination started working, and even though I wasn't planning on buying a new car for at least six months, my faith was activated. I stayed up most of that night trying to figure out how Jamie and I could afford it!

Your imagination activates your faith. If you're believing for healing but haven't paused to "see" yourself healed, you don't have a faith problem; you have a thermostat problem. And unless you first begin to hope—to use your imagination in a positive way—the power unit of faith will not turn on.

I once read the following quote by T. E. Lawrence (Lawrence of Arabia): "All men dream: but not equally. Those who dream by night in the dusty recesses of their minds wake in the day to find that it was vanity: but the dreamers of the day are dangerous men, for they may act their dream with open eyes, to make it possible." You see, people who dream—people who see with their hearts—are the people who change the world.

Chapter 17

FAITH'S PARTNER

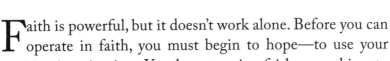

Faith is powerful, but it doesn't work alone. Before you can operate in faith, you must begin to hope—to use your positive imagination. You have to give faith something to work with.

I remember when our ministry was still very small. We had less than thirty employees and around 2,500 partners. We were struggling. It looked like we were going under. My staff kept coming to me saying, "You have to tell people. You have to share this need with your partners." But I just didn't know what to say. Then I had a dream. In the dream, a partner from Dallas, Texas, approached me to ask how I was doing. "I'm blessed," I answered.

"I know you're blessed, Andrew," he said. "But I want to know about your finances."

"Well, to be honest," I said, "we're struggling." And I told him about the ministry's financial situation.

He got mad—really mad—at me! "God raised me up to be your partner!" he said. "How can I do what God has called me to do and help you when you won't give me the information I need?"

I didn't know what to say. He continued, "Your pride is keeping you from telling people what's going on."

Brothers and sisters, I woke up with a word from God! I wrote a letter to my partners immediately. In the letter, I shared my dream, repented, and told them about our financial need. I didn't ask them to give. I didn't even include a return envelope, but within ten days, the ministry received $53,000—at that time, nearly a year's worth of income.

That dream ignited my hope. It gave me something to aim for, something for my faith to grab hold of.

It's important that you don't skip this step and that you give faith something to work with. Meditate on the Word. Seek out people who will encourage you. Open your heart to testimonies of others who have experienced victory over similar challenges.

I remember a testimony from a lady from Mobile, Alabama, who'd basically lived out of her chair for years, crippled with arthritis—until the day her husband saw me on television. I was teaching on *The Believer's Authority*, and he asked her to watch with him. She agreed. After the program, her husband turned to her and told her to stand up. Nervously, she stood. Within moments, this woman, who had been considering double-knee replacement surgery to deal with her arthritic pain, took off running in her nightgown! She ran out of the house and down the street, completely healed. When she got back to the house, she found her husband lying on the floor. She thought he'd died of a heart attack, but he was just stretched out under the power of God! She wrote to us, praising God for the ability to enjoy life. She said she regularly plays racquetball and swims.

My ministry website is full of testimonies like this, and new ones come in all the time. We have testimonies from people healed of cancer, fibromyalgia, autism, and other "incurable" diseases. We have testimonies from people who've discovered their purpose and from others who have experienced protection, provision, and freedom. But every-one started with a hopeful imagination.

Don't disparage hope. Hope is not the end result; it is faith's partner. It is a step in the process. Hope gives your faith something to work for!

Christians get so excited over miracles and discoveries that "prove" the Bible is real. They think if we give unbelievers enough physical evidence, they will be converted. The problem is, faith doesn't come through physical, tangible evidence. Faith only comes by hearing the Word of God (Rom. 10:17). You can't argue a person into faith. You can't make them believe. Archeological finds, scientific discoveries, and miracles don't produce faith. They produce hope. They get people's attention and give them something to consider.

Jesus told a story in Luke 16 about two men who died. One was a rich man who spent his life living for himself and went to hell. The other was a man named Lazarus, and he joined the righteous in Abraham's bosom. (Abraham's bosom was like a holding place for those who died in faith looking forward to the coming of the Messiah. Since Jesus had not yet dealt with sin through His death and resurrection, these Old Testament men and women could not enter heaven. They had to wait for Jesus to provide access to the Father. They had to wait for the new birth.) While in hell, the rich man suffered greatly. He called across the gulf and asked Abraham to send Lazarus back to earth to warn his brothers. Abraham responded:

> *They have Moses and the prophets; let them hear them. And he said, Nay, father Abraham: but if one went unto them from the dead, they will repent. And he said unto him, If they hear not Moses and the prophets, neither will they be persuaded, though one rose from the dead.*

Luke 16:29-31

Abraham told this rich man that if his brothers didn't believe the Word, they wouldn't believe even if someone was raised from the dead. Faith only comes by hearing the Word of God (Rom. 10:17).

Physical evidence doesn't produce faith. People who need physical evidence to believe are carnal, and without intervention, they will struggle to receive from God. To receive from

God, the Word has to become more to us than just ink on a page. It has to come alive in our hearts. We can't just read the Bible and expect it to produce fruit in our lives. We have to conceive it; we have to spend time thinking about it and letting it become a part of who we are.

You may have noticed, but I rarely use notes when I minister. Occasionally I'll write down Greek words or definitions, but in general, I don't use notes. I don't need to. I know the Word. It's not just something I study. I've spent so many years meditating on Scripture—thinking on it, imagining it—that it's become a part of me.

For example, I don't struggle remembering the day Jamie and I got married—I was there. Our ceremony lasted an hour and forty-five minutes. There was preaching, singing, and an invitation. Our recessional song was Handel's *Hallelujah Chorus*. If you were to ask me about the ceremony, I wouldn't need to "pray about it" for a week. I wouldn't need to get out my notes or review our wedding album. I was there. It was very real to me. I remember it vividly.

I never study the Bible to get something for others. I never "prepare" a message for someone else. I study for me. I read the Word and meditate on it until God does something in me. Once it's become real to me, messages are easy. I simply share with you what God has already told me. It's like one beggar telling another beggar where to find a free meal. I can tell you about healing because I've been healed. I can tell you about prosperity because I've been prospered. I can tell you that the

Word works because I've seen it. I can tell you about using your imagination because I've lived it.

Years ago at a Charis Campus Days event, I was sitting in my usual spot (the front row along the aisle) with my eyes closed, listening to my wife lead praise and worship. The place we met that year was set up with a center aisle and had double doors on the side. As Jamie and the crowd were singing, suddenly, in my mind's eye, I saw the double doors fly open. I saw Jesus walk through the doors and let them gently close behind Him. I kept watching (with my eyes closed) as He walked over and touched a lady on the front row. She fell on her face. Then Jesus walked past two people and touched another woman on the head. She hit her knees with her hands in the air, worshiping God. It all seemed so real that I opened my eyes and looked toward the doors.

Immediately the doors flew open—just like I'd seen in my imagination. But Jesus wasn't there. I kept watching as the doors closed, and I saw the first woman fall to the floor. A few moments later, the other woman hit her knees. Everything I had seen in my heart was happening right before my eyes. The only difference was, I couldn't see the spiritual things—only the physical. I realized I had been seeing things better with my heart, so I closed my eyes again and watched as the Lord approached me.

He laid his hands on me and answered many of the questions I'd been wrestling with. Then He started walking down the aisle, touching people and speaking to them. When the service was over, I approached several of the people I knew

Jesus had spoken to and asked them what had happened. They told me the exact same things I'd heard the Lord tell them in my imagination.

God created us to live at a higher level than we do. Most of us go through life half-blind, seeing only with our physical eyes. And just like a blind person is limited in what they can experience in life, we who walk through this life without using our imaginations are limited.

Chapter 18

HOPE COMES FROM RELATIONSHIP

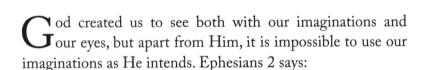

G od created us to see both with our imaginations and
our eyes, but apart from Him, it is impossible to use our
imaginations as He intends. Ephesians 2 says:

> *And you hath he quickened, who were dead in tres-*
> *passes and sins; Wherein in time past ye walked*
> *according to the course of this world, according to*
> *the prince of the power of the air, the spirit that*
> *now worketh in the children of disobedience:*
> *Among whom also we all had our conversation*
> *in times past in the lusts of our flesh, fulfilling the*
> *desires of the flesh and of the mind; and were by*
> *nature the children of wrath, even as others.*
>
> **Ephesians 2:1-3**

Paul said that before Christ, we were children of the devil by nature. We were disobedient and selfish, living only to satisfy the *"lusts of our flesh."* Most people don't like to hear this. They want to believe they are good people and that Jesus is just the icing on the cake. But there are no good people. (I know that's offensive, but it's true.) There are just varying degrees of being lost. Scripture says we were *all* dead in trespasses and sins. We've all fallen short of God's standard (Rom. 3:23). People who aren't born again are children of wrath by nature; the spirit of disobedience works in them. That's who we all were prior to surrendering to Christ.

Many in our society refuse to acknowledge this. They refuse to admit that they are selfish, that without Christ they have no hope. They say, "I may not be as good as I'm supposed to be, but I'm pretty good." But who wants to be the best sinner who went to hell? Second Corinthians 10:12 says that comparing ourselves among ourselves and measuring ourselves by ourselves is not wise. Maybe you haven't robbed, raped, or killed, but I guarantee that you've been selfish or have hurt others. All of us have sinned; we all need a Savior. If we're not willing to acknowledge that, then we can't be saved.

When the United States was formed, our Founding Fathers believed that mankind was inherently evil and selfish. They believed that, left to ourselves, we would suppress and destroy one another. So, they set down laws—in keeping with biblical morality—to curb that desire. Yet today, I would be castigated for saying such things. People would take offense. But that's exactly what the Bible says.

The heart is deceitful above all things, and desperately wicked: who can know it?

Jeremiah 17:9

Without Christ, we are selfish. God is the only good thing in our lives (Luke 18:19). Anyone who thinks otherwise is deceived.

Salvation is not based on our goodness. Many people think that if their good deeds outweigh their bad, God will accept them. But if we keep the whole Law and yet offend in one point, we become guilty of breaking it all (James 2:10). God never compares us to other people. He doesn't grade on a curve. His standard is Jesus. If we aren't as perfect and as pure as Jesus, we fail. We need a Savior.

Good people don't go to heaven, and bad people don't go to hell. Only forgiven people go to heaven, and only those who do not accept the Lord's forgiveness go to hell.

You know, I've lived a relatively good life. I've not broken "the big ten." I've never taken a drink of liquor. I've never smoked a cigarette. I've never even tasted coffee. Compared to most people reading this book, I've lived a super holy life. But I've still sinned; I've still fallen short of God's standard. I don't need Jesus to just make up the deficit. Compared to Him, all my goodness is *"as filthy rags"* (Is. 64:6). I need mercy.

I used to develop pictures for a living. Often when we took pictures of women and showed them the proofs, they'd say, "I look terrible. My hair is out of place. My makeup is smudged.

This doesn't do me justice." Most times I think they were just fishing for a compliment, but there were a few times I wanted to say "Lady, you don't need justice. You need mercy!"

Likewise, brothers and sisters, no matter how "good" we think we've been, we don't want justice. If we were to get what we deserved, every one of us would go to hell. We all need mercy. We don't need Muhammad. We can't get to God through Buddha. We need Jesus.

Christianity is the only religion on the face of the planet that has a Savior. In every other religion, salvation is earned by what you do. Christianity is not about what you do; it's about what was done *for* you. Because of Jesus, we are no longer alienated from God. We now have access to the covenants of promise, and we can now experience hope—a positive imagination—in this world.

Paul went on to say in Ephesians that because of God's great love, He had mercy on us (Eph. 2:4). He *"quickened us"* and made us alive with Christ (Eph. 2:5). Paul said we were born again by grace through faith (Eph. 2:8). Then he said:

> *Wherefore remember, that ye being in time past Gentiles in the flesh, who are called Uncircumcision by that which is called the Circumcision in the flesh made by hands; That at that time ye were without Christ, being aliens from the commonwealth of Israel, and strangers from the covenants of promise, having no hope, and without God in the world.*
>
> **Ephesians 2:11-12**

These verses are comparing the Jews, God's chosen people, with everyone else on the face of the earth, otherwise known as Gentiles. This might be easier to understand if we relate it to those who are born again and have become a part of God's family and those who haven't. These verses say that without Christ, we are alienated from the life of God. Outside of Christ, the promises in God's Word do not apply to us, and we have no hope. That's why Jesus said, *"I am the way, the truth, and the life: no man cometh unto the Father, but by me"* (John 14:6).

Relationship with God gives us hope. When Jamie and I received word that our son was dead, he had already been dead for several hours. The circumstance we were facing looked and felt hopeless. Yet I remember driving into town praying, "Father, You're a good God. I know You didn't kill my son. I know this is not Your will. I love You, Lord, and I want You to know that no matter what happens, I will continue to serve You." I didn't feel like praising God in that moment. I felt like crying. But as I made the decision to praise, the Lord brought to my remembrance a word He'd spoken to me.

Years before, while Jamie and I were ministering in Ireland, a lady who didn't know anything about our family approached us and said, "You have two boys, and the younger will return to the Lord and serve Him before the older." Later that same year, in California, a stranger approached me in the prayer line at one of my meetings and said, "You have two boys, and the younger will serve the Lord before the older." Two different people on two different continents, who'd never met one another and didn't know me, prophesied the exact same word. When I chose to trust God the day my son died, He reminded me of those prophecies—and hope came alive! My younger son hadn't yet returned to the Lord, so in order for those words to be fulfilled, my son would have to live! I began laughing and told Jamie, "This is going to be the greatest miracle we've ever seen!"

My relationship with God gave me hope in that situation. It anchored my soul when nothing around me appeared solid. That hope ignited my faith, and we saw our son live!

Chapter 19

PERSPECTIVE

Hope (a positive imagination) is the antidote for depression.

I read an article on an airplane once that said people who smile more often are happier people than those who don't smile. According to the article, psychologists actually researched why people who smile are happier than people who frown. I got so mad when I read their conclusion. They said that smiling more makes a person happier. How dumb can you get and still breathe? It's not smiling that makes a person happy. It's being happy that makes a person smile. Those geniuses couldn't figure that out. And they spent millions of taxpayer dollars to come to that conclusion.

We get things so mixed up. We treat the symptoms instead of the cause.

A man once came to me who was manic-depressive and struggling with suicidal thoughts. He said, "I can't help it. I have no control over my emotions. Please pray that God would do something!"

"No," I said. "You're denying what the Word says; you've got the wrong perspective. I'm not going to pray and agree with you about this or we'd both be wrong."

"What do you mean?" he asked.

"The Bible says to resist the devil and he will flee from you," I said. "You're telling me that you resisted the devil and he *didn't* flee. So, you're saying that the Word of God didn't work. That's wrong. You have the authority and power to overcome this, but you're in unbelief. To say there is nothing you can do is completely wrong. You can control your emotions."

"Oh no," he said. "I'm manic-depressive. I have to take pills to control myself."

"There is nothing wrong with you," I told him. "Your emotions work perfectly."

"No, they don't. I'm depressed all day long."

"Your emotions work just fine," I said again. "They follow your thoughts. It's your thoughts that are wrong, not your emotions."

Brothers and sisters, you cannot be hopeful and depressed at the same time. If you're depressed, it's because you aren't hoping. You aren't imagining the Word. You don't know what your relationship with God has provided you. You are looking at the world and listening to the world. You're seeing and anticipating negative things. It's not what happens to you that dictates your emotions; it's how you perceive what happens that affects you.

For instance, take two siblings from the same gene pool, raised in the exact same alcoholic environment. This identical situation can produce two very different responses. One sibling can end up becoming an alcoholic, while the other never touches the stuff.

I remember the first time I heard the testimony of Connie Weiskopf. She said that when she developed cancer, all her friends told her to learn everything she could about the disease so she would know how to fight it. But the Lord spoke to her, saying, "No, you don't need to learn everything about cancer. You need to learn everything you can about healing."

God didn't want Connie's emotions to run away with her. He didn't want her studying all the ways cancer could kill her. That would have painted a negative picture in her imagination. Connie grabbed hold of God's Word and began listening to my teachings. She started meditating on healing. And she was healed!

If you had a positive imagination based on God's Word, no matter what came knocking on your door or what your circumstances looked like, you could respond like Connie and like the psalmist:

> *Why art thou cast down, O my soul? and why art*
> *thou disquieted in me? hope thou in God: for I shall*
> *yet praise him for the help of his countenance. . . .*
> *Why art thou cast down, O my soul? and why art*

> *thou disquieted within me? hope thou in God: for I*
> *shall yet praise him, who is the health of my coun-*
> *tenance, and my God.*

Psalm 42:5, 11

The writer of this psalm, King David, took control of his emotions. He chose to set his hope (his positive imagination) on God, even though his soul felt *"disquieted."* He chose to remember who God is and to praise Him for being his help and health.

Second Corinthians 2:14 says that God always causes us to triumph in Christ. If we hoped that this verse was true, if we began to picture it coming to pass in our lives, I guarantee that faith would follow. We wouldn't be depressed. We wouldn't worry. We wouldn't allow problems to discourage us. And we would see this Scripture fulfilled in our lives.

We were created by God. Within each of us is a God-like part that has His nature. And like Him, we can control ourselves. We can control our emotions. If we couldn't, the Lord would have been unjust to tell His disciples to *"let not your heart be troubled"* the night before His crucifixion (John 14:1).

Jesus had actually told His disciples fourteen different times that He would be crucified and would rise again. Then Jesus commanded them twice in one night not to let their hearts be troubled.

> *Let not your heart be troubled: ye believe in God,*
> *believe also in me.*

John 14:1

These things I have spoken unto you, that in me ye might have peace. In the world ye shall have tribulation: but be of good cheer; I have overcome the world.

John 16:33

Modern psychology would call that unreasonable. Political correctness would berate Jesus for not embracing His disciples' "truth." After all, they were going to see Him beaten and rejected. They would witness Him being mocked and spit upon. They would see Him crucified and buried. It was only natural that they should feel "troubled"; they would have been in denial if they hadn't. But if Jesus's disciples had put hope in what He said, they wouldn't have been troubled.

"You can have peace," Jesus told them. "In this world you will have trouble, but because I have overcome, you can still experience peace, even in trouble." (John 16:33) If you could see yourself in Christ and Christ in you, it would change your attitude.

In Ephesians 1:18, Paul prayed that we would *"know what is the hope of his calling, and what the riches of the glory of his inheritance in the saints."* The glory of Christ's inheritance is in us—in the saints. When most people think about glory, they think about Old Testament pictures that compare God's glory to a thick cloud that was so overwhelming, the priests couldn't minister. People equate God's glory with His presence or power, and while it certainly includes that, it is much more. God's glory is everything He is; it's not just what He looks or sounds like. God's glory encompasses His nature, His goodness, His wisdom, His worth, and all that He does. Scripture tells us that the glory of God is Christ Jesus (2 Cor. 4:6 and Heb. 1:3). But just look at what Jesus said:

> *And the glory which thou gavest me I have given them; that they may be one, even as we are one.*

> ### John 17:22

The glory of God—the person of Jesus—lives in us. If we somehow or other "lost" that glory and it had to be replaced, it would bankrupt heaven (Rom. 8:18). That's how awesome God's glory in us is! Yet many Christians don't think this verse could possibly apply to them. They couldn't possibly have the glory of God dwelling in them; all they see are gray hair, wrinkles, and bulges. They remember the words they said ten years ago or the thoughts they had last week. They don't understand the process of *"obtaining of the glory of our Lord"* (2 Thess. 2:14). They don't understand spirit, soul, and body.

Every believer who's suffering with sickness and disease, struggling with addiction and fear, or living a defeated life literally couldn't be closer to God's raising-from-the-dead power. It's right inside them. But people struggle with this teaching. They think I'm telling hurting people that they shouldn't be hurting. They think I'm not being compassionate. I understand there is pain in this world. I understand we all face uncomfortable circumstances, that there are reasons people hurt. But sometimes the best thing I can do is encourage people to come up higher—to rise up above their circumstances.

A friend of mine, Dave Duell, once told a couple who came for prayer, "Thus saith the Lord, 'My little children, don't feel bad. If I weren't God, I'd be discouraged too.'" They didn't care for that very much. They wanted Dave to wallow with them in their sorrow and depression. But God wasn't wringing His hands. He wasn't worried about their problem, so neither was Dave. He knew their issue wouldn't be such a drain on God's power that it would dim the lights in heaven. He knew that God's power was more than enough to meet their need.

When Ashley and Carlie Terradez were believing God for their daughter's healing, I remember telling them, "That's a piece of cake for Jesus!" At the time, their daughter was three years old. She had never eaten solid foods. She had to be fed through a tube inserted into her belly. She wore nine-month-old baby clothes, couldn't control her bowels, was losing her hair, and slept much of the day. Before, when they shared their daughter's illness with people, all they received were words of sympathy and disbelief. My "That's no big deal" attitude sparked their faith, and their daughter was instantly healed when I prayed for her. They've been living in victory over eosinophilic enteropathy, the autoimmune disease their daughter had, for more than ten years!

We don't have to live defeated, discouraged lives. God always causes us to triumph in Christ! But we have to cooperate with Him. We have to pull our thumbs out of our mouths, put on our big-boy or big-girl pants, and engage our imaginations.

Chapter 20

CONCEPTION PROCESS

Hope is a powerful force, one our society and many in the church have abandoned. I go into Spirit-filled churches all the time and am shocked at the number of people who say they're fighting depression. They've allowed themselves to be so immersed in the world's system that they're now drowning in it.

I once saw a bumper sticker that read "If you aren't depressed, you aren't paying attention." And that's true if we only look at things in the natural. Life is a terminal experience. We're all going to die eventually (if Jesus doesn't come back in our lifetime). The world doesn't want us to hope. The media covers only bad news. Politicians and pundits rely on worst-case scenarios to drive votes. Doctors go out of their way to not get people's hopes up. To the world, hope is a liability.

There's a tendency for ministers to have the same attitude. I pray for people all the time who say they're healed but then ask, "Should I quit my medicine?" That puts me in a tough spot. I can't see their faith. I don't know their heart. What if they aren't really believing? What if they've put the cart before the horse and are counting on their actions to produce faith? What if I say "Quit your medicine," and their quitting proves they weren't in faith? I'm left holding the bag.

When someone asks me "Should I quit my medicine?" I say, "Ask the Holy Spirit. That's what He's for." Other people can't operate on my faith. People who take medication do so because they believe they're sick and that the medicine will help. I don't take medication because I don't believe I'm sick. If you believe you're sick, maybe you should take medicine. If you believe you're healed, you may not need meds; you may just need to wait for a manifestation or wean yourself off them slowly. I don't know what's in your heart. I don't know what's going on in your body. You need to pray for wisdom and listen to what the Holy Spirit tells you.

I'm not against medicine. I'm not against doctors or veterinarians. But I wouldn't take my dog to a vet—because I don't have a dog! If you have a dog, you may need to take it to the vet from time to time. You have to do what you have faith to do. Don't try to operate at someone else's level of faith. Don't try to "fake it till you make it." If you don't yet have faith, start the process by hoping.

This world is a depressing place, but we as believers share in the *"blessed hope"* (Titus 2:13). We have a promise that this life isn't all there is, that all God's promises are yes and amen in Christ (2 Cor. 1:20). We have reason to hope! But we have to encourage ourselves in the Lord (1 Sam. 30:6). We have to use our imaginations to meditate on God's Word and picture the Word coming to pass in our lives.

Your imagination is your spiritual womb. The Word of God is a seed (1 Pet. 1:23). It's like a sperm that when planted in your heart—your imagination—will begin the process of conception. Most Christians don't understand this. When they have a problem, they go to God begging and pleading for Him to move. They tell others of their desperation and pray for a miracle, but they're praying in unbelief. And while God certainly works miracles, miracles don't come from the outside in. They come from the inside out. God created us to conceive miracles in our imaginations.

When we take the seed of God's Word and plant it in our spiritual wombs, conception occurs. But there is a waiting period involved before manifestation, in the same way that a pregnant woman has to nurture a child for nine months before she can give birth. The woman may not even realize she's pregnant in the beginning of the process, but her child is no less real. She is no less pregnant.

In the spiritual realm, it may take a period of time after you conceive before you feel like anything is happening. That's okay. Continue to nurture that seed. Before long, you'll start noticing change, and if you keep at it, so will everyone else! They'll start encouraging you, believing with you. And when you give birth to your miracle, they'll say, "Praise God! That was quick!" But like a woman giving birth to a child, you'll know you incubated that miracle for nine months. You conceived it long before.

Many of us want to give birth to a miracle or see God's will in our lives, but our imaginations have never had intercourse with the Word. People look at me and see what's happening in the ministry and see the blessing and favor I'm receiving and think, *If Andrew can do it, so can I. I'm going to believe God for that.* And that's wonderful—God is no respecter of persons (Rom. 2:11). But they don't realize how many years I've been incubating these dreams. They don't see the years of faithful sowing and directing my imagination that it took to get me where I am today. A few years ago, someone gave me a brand-new Cadillac Escalade. It's a blessing! But if one of my students saw that car and decided to believe God for one, it might be a period of time before they saw that desire fulfilled. They'd have to hold on to hope, allow their imagination to conceive, and keep nurturing that seed until the fulfillment came. Most people would give up (Prov. 13:12).

"What if it takes me a year?" someone may ask. Well, it took me forty-eight years. But you can't get there any quicker than if you start today. Start the process. Let God plant a dream in your heart. Meditate on it until you conceive. I promise you will see the fulfillment of that dream if you don't give up.

You might be thinking, *I don't have that kind of time. I'm not a full-time minister. I can't meditate all day. I don't have time to daydream.*

But you meditate all the time; you just don't realize it. Meditation is simply keeping your mind focused. Worry is meditation. Worry is thinking about something and seeing something that hasn't happened. It's exploring negative possibilities. You worry about your finances, about your kids, about your marriage. You worry all day long and still manage to do your job.

Likewise, you can meditate on the positive all day long. It just takes practice. Take a Scripture from God's Word and just keep your mind focused on it. Picture what that Scripture would look like in your own life. Think of others who've seen the truth of that word work. Ponder what the author of that Scripture was thinking when they wrote it. Ask questions about it. That's how the Word comes alive.

I meditate on the Word constantly. I don't always have time to read it, but I live my life focused on God's Word, and it's working! I live in health. I am prosperous. I have peace. I'm not saying I do this perfectly—because I certainly don't—but to the degree that I seek the Lord and keep my imagination focused on Him, I have peace (Is. 26:3).

Brothers and sisters, our future is so bright we've got to squint to look at it! God has provided everything we need. But it has to get from our spirits and through our minds before we can see it manifest in our bodies. Romans 12:2 says:

> *And be not conformed to this world: but be ye transformed by the renewing of your mind, that ye may prove what is that good, and acceptable, and perfect, will of God.*

The *New Living Translation* renders Romans 12:2 like this:

> *Don't copy the behavior and customs of this world, but let God transform you into a new person by changing the way you think. Then you will learn to know God's will for you, which is good and pleasing and perfect.*

The Word of God is so valuable! It gives us God's thoughts. It shows us God's way of looking at things. Too often we allow our minds to be polluted. We conform—if not our behavior, then our thoughts—to the way the world thinks. But God has given us the seed of His Word to meet every need in our lives. We just have to conceive it.

Chapter 21

BEATING SIN AT CONCEPTION

Our born-again spirits are 100 percent righteous and holy (Eph. 4:24). We have the mind of Christ (1 Cor. 2:16). Our spirits are full of love, joy, peace, patience, self-control, and every other fruit of the Spirit (Gal. 5:22-23). Our spirits are complete in Christ (Col. 2:10). We can't get any more saved. We can't become more perfect (Heb. 10:14). The rest of our Christian lives is about learning how to turn these spiritual realities into natural realities.

Many people say to me, "I just don't feel the love of God. Would you please pray that God would release His love toward me?" But God has already poured out His love toward us. He proved His love for us 2,000 years ago in the person of Jesus (Rom. 5:5-8). How much more love can He give? We're not waiting on God to show us His love. We simply need to notify our brains of what He has already done! That's what these verses are talking about:

> *According as his divine power hath given unto us all things that pertain unto life and godliness, through the knowledge of him that hath called us to glory and virtue.*

> **2 Peter 1:3**

> *That the communication of thy faith may become effectual by the acknowledging of every good thing which is in you in Christ Jesus.*

> **Philemon 6**

When we renew our minds to spiritual truth, we begin to see the life of God made manifest. We begin to see our faith work.

I heard that during Abraham Lincoln's presidency, when he signed the Emancipation Proclamation to free slaves in America, many slave owners hid the news from their households. There are documented cases of freed slaves continuing in bondage simply because they were ignorant of the freedom extended to them.

Satan has been doing the same thing to the church for centuries. When we don't know who we are or what we have in

Christ, we can't move those spiritual realities into the natural realm (Hos. 4:6).

Imagine a pipe that connects the resurrection power of God to your sickness, poverty, depression, or discouragement. On one end of the pipe is a reservoir of power. On the other, your need. In the middle of the pipe is a valve, which represents your soul. Nothing can come through that valve until your imagination is in line with God and His Word. You can go through life completely shut off from the life-giving power of God if you don't take time to renew your mind.

> *That ye put off concerning the former conversation* [the old way of living and thinking] *the old man, which is corrupt according to the deceitful lusts; And be renewed in the spirit* [attitude] *of your mind; And that ye put on the new man, which after God is created in righteousness and true holiness.*
>
> **Ephesians 4:22-24, brackets added**

When I was drafted into the Vietnam War at the age of nineteen, my identity in Christ was put to the test. I had just received a revelation of God's love that changed my life, but I wasn't in Texas anymore. Out of my entire company in Vietnam, I was the only person who was a Christian. There may have been others, but if there were, they were in hiding. One of the bunkers I was assigned to on a fire support base was wallpapered with nude pictures. You couldn't look anywhere—at the walls, the ceiling, anywhere—without seeing a naked woman. Dope was free and vulgarity was rampant. It was terrible. It was also like a magnet pulling me toward sin.

I remember my first stand-down. In times of war, combat units that see a lot of action are given reprieve days away from the battlefield. These days are supposed to be morale boosters, times for troops to take care of personal needs, receive medical care, and call home. Well, the government ordered us to have three days of "stand-down" and paid for all the free booze and sex a man could want. They brought in Filipino prostitutes and strippers and for three days sponsored an orgy. I was the only man in my division who didn't participate. Even the chaplain joined in. I remember thinking, *Am I the only one who fears God?*

The only way I survived Vietnam was with my nose in the Bible. Fifteen hours a day (when I wasn't in a foxhole or pointing a gun), I'd read. I couldn't even put the Bible down to think. If I did, I'd see nudity. I didn't realize at the time what was happening (I was just reading out of desperation), but the Word began painting a picture inside me. It began to change the way I thought.

I was so in love with the Lord and focused on Him during my time in Vietnam that it was like I was in a bubble. Nothing fazed me. One day I was in a situation where it looked like we would certainly die. We took scores of mortar hits on our position, and I could see the muzzle fire from the enemies' guns. But all I could think about was that I might see Jesus face-to-face before the day was over. I was actually rejoicing in the Lord.

I started praying for the enemy soldiers who were firing on us. I knew where I would go if I died, but what about them? I actually felt the love of the Lord flowing out of me toward them as I had my M-16 pointed at them.

I know you might think that's weird. Well, I admit it's certainly not what most soldiers experienced, but it's not weird at all if you have been meditating on God's Word as Paul did. He said that he would rather go be with the Lord than live in his body (Phil. 1:20-23). The only reason he stayed in this life was because of the benefit it would be to others. If we thought properly about things, we would rejoice at the thought of heaven, regardless of how we got there.

Your imagination and the way you think and respond to circumstances is vital. God—by grace—has provided everything you need for life and godliness (2 Pet. 1:3). He has already blessed you with all spiritual blessings in Christ (Eph. 1:3). But you have to take the seed of His Word, plant it in your imagination, and let it germinate so that you can conceive victory. It really is as simple as I've described. But renewing your mind is also the hardest thing you'll ever do.

We're surrounded by ungodliness, by secular, humanistic thinking. Every day thousands of babies are killed on the altar of convenience. Every day people are dying, starving, and hurting because of other people's selfish actions. Our society celebrates and excuses sin in the name of "love" and "tolerance." Our culture is antagonistic toward Christianity and biblical values. And if you don't stick your nose in the Bible and allow the Word to change your imagination, you will be sucked in. You will be swallowed up.

You can't read the Bible for fifteen hours a day and not see change. You can't watch four or five years' worth of healing testimonies on our website and stay sick. Brothers and sisters, God is not the one at fault. We have hardened our hearts. We have allowed ourselves to be influenced by ungodliness, to be conformed to the world's way of thinking and doing. But we can change it. We can change our imaginations.

Hundreds of people died to preserve us a translation of the Bible. William Tyndale, one of the first men to translate the Bible into English, was burned at the stake. But his death wasn't in vain. Less than seventy years later, King James authorized a translation of the Bible due, in large part, to the outcry of the people who witnessed Tyndale's death.

Throughout history, people have sacrificed their own lives to ensure we have a copy of the Scriptures, and I daresay the average Christian takes that for granted. Most don't open the Bible except on Sundays, or if they do, it's for a two-minute devotional. Christians spend two minutes reading God's Word and the rest of the day watching "As the Stomach Turns." Yet they wonder why things aren't working.

Most Christians are having daily intercourse with the world and then hoping for a spiritual abortion or miscarriage to keep from giving birth to sin and negativity. I remember the advice my Uncle Saffie gave me when Jamie and I got married. He took me aside and told me, in his homespun way, "Boy, you're a Wommack. Wommacks don't get divorced. This isn't Sears and Roebuck. If you don't like her, you can't bring her back." In other words, *Be sure you're making a good decision, 'cause you have to live with the consequences!* Jamie and I both entered our marriage with this perspective, and we've never thought about divorce. We've thought about murder a few times (just kidding), but we've never spoken of divorce and never threatened it.

I'm not sure how many reading this book could say the same. Some of you threaten your spouse with divorce and separation. You use those threats as leverage to get your way. That's the world's way of thinking. But if you understood what I am talking about, you would never go there. You would understand the damage those words and thoughts produce. You wouldn't want that image in your imagination or your spouse's.

In this and other areas, we as believers try to stop the action of sin, but we don't take responsibility for the conception of it. It's like a woman going out and sleeping with a different man every night and never expecting to get pregnant. That's not the way it works. It's not hard to avoid giving birth—simply stop conceiving.

The Word tells us to be *"wise unto that which is good, and simple concerning evil"* (Rom. 16:19). The word translated *"simple"* here means "innocent" (*Strong's Concordance*). And Ephesians 5:11-12 says, *"Have no fellowship with the unfruitful works of darkness, but rather reprove them. For it is a shame even to speak of those things which are done of them in secret."* The Word says we shouldn't even talk about evil, yet many Christians pipe it into their homes. They turn on the television and watch murder, lying, adultery, lust, and fornication. And given enough time, those images will produce fruit in their lives.

Brothers and sisters, God's way is much better! Learn to control your imagination, and avoid sin altogether!

Chapter 22

SPEAKING INTO YOUR FUTURE

If I were to ask you to pray for a future generation, what would you pray? What would you see as their most pressing need? And if I were to ask you to write that prayer down, what would you record? How would you encourage people not yet born to praise the Lord (Ps. 102:18)?

I can imagine how that prayer would go, because I've heard the prayers of hundreds of people praying for others. It would go something like "O God, just pour out Your Spirit on those people. Let them have a new touch from You. Send them revival. Do a *new* thing . . ."

Here's how Apostle Paul prayed for others:

Wherefore I also, after I heard of your faith in the Lord Jesus, and love unto all the saints, Cease not to give thanks for you, making mention of you in my prayers; That the God of our Lord Jesus Christ, the Father of glory, may give unto you the spirit of wisdom and revelation in the knowledge of him: The eyes of your understanding being enlightened; that ye may know what is the hope of his calling, and what the riches of the glory of his inheritance in the saints, And what is the exceeding greatness of his power to us-ward who believe, according to the working of his mighty power, Which he wrought in Christ, when he raised him from the dead, and set him at his own right hand in the heavenly places, Far above all principality, and power, and might, and dominion, and every name that is named, not only in this world, but also in that which is to come: And hath put all things under his feet, and gave him to be the head over all things to the church, Which is his body, the fulness of him that filleth all in all.

Ephesians 1:15-23

Paul didn't pray that you and I would get something new; he prayed that we would get a revelation of what we already have. Paul prayed that the *"eyes of* [our] *understanding"* (brackets added) would be enlightened. The word translated *"understanding"* here is the Greek word *dianoia*. Remember, *dianoia* means deep thought. Paul prayed that our understanding—our deep thought—would be opened to help us see *"the hope of his calling"* and receive from God. That's speaking about getting a picture in our imaginations of what God has for us.

As a believer, you are a partner with God—a partaker of His nature, of what He is doing on the earth (2 Pet. 1:4 and Heb. 3:1). Get a picture of that! God is asking you to do something bigger than yourself. He's asking you to join in what He's doing. You are the body of Christ (1 Cor. 12:27). You are His hands and feet, His minister—whether you work in the secular world or in the church. You get to do the works He did and even *"greater works"* (John 14:12). But to become an effective partner, you need to engage your imagination.

Without your imagination, you won't be able to understand *"the riches of the glory of his inheritance"* within you (Eph. 1:18). You won't be able to experience the *"exceeding greatness of his power"* (Eph. 1:19). Those words *"exceeding greatness"* are hyperbole. They emphasize the fact that God's power toward you is infinitely greater than anything you could imagine (Eph. 3:20). It's the same power He *"wrought in Christ, when he raised him from the dead"* (Eph. 1:20). If you could hook up a volume-unit (VU) meter to the power of God to gauge its potency, I believe you'd find that creating the world took less power than raising Jesus from the dead. When God created the universe, He had zero opposition. But when He raised Jesus from the dead, Satan and every demon in hell was trying to stop Him. Of course, they couldn't. But the point is, it took more power to raise Jesus from the dead than it did to create the entire universe. And that same creative, raising-from-the-dead power is on the inside of you!

Paul prayed that our eyes would be opened, that our imaginations would understand all that God has given us in Christ and the enormity of the power He's placed within us to do what He's called us to do—to be His partners, His hands and feet in the earth. Man, that's awesome!

Most people don't pray like this. Most Christians I've encountered would pray for the next generation by asking God to do something new. But 2,000 years ago, the man who wrote nearly half the books in the New Testament prayed that we would recognize all that God has already done for us in Christ and know the *"exceeding greatness of his power"* (Eph. 1:19) within us. Paul prayed that God would show us what we already have.

Just a few verses before, in Ephesians 1:8, Paul said that God *"hath abounded toward us in all wisdom and prudence."* Notice the word *"hath"*—past tense. It's already done. So, when Paul prayed that God would give us the *"spirit of wisdom and revelation"* (Eph. 1:17), he was really praying that God would help us understand what we already have.

> *Blessed be the God and Father of our Lord Jesus Christ, who hath blessed us with all spiritual blessings in heavenly places in Christ.*
>
> **Ephesians 1:3**

The entire Christian world seems to be stuck in a constant state of begging God to do something He hasn't done. But the truth is, God has already blessed us with all spiritual blessings in Christ. If someone needs to be born again, Jesus doesn't have to die again. He already did that. He already paid the price for sin (Heb. 9:28). If someone needs healing, that's done too. First Peter 2:24 says, *"By whose stripes ye were healed"*—past tense. If someone needs wisdom, Ephesians 1:8 says that the Father *"hath abounded toward us in all wisdom and prudence."* God has already provided for our every need.

Creation is a good example. Though man was the crowning jewel of all God's creation, He didn't create man first. If He had, man would have been treading water for four days, waiting for land to appear. Man would've had to dodge trees and mountains as they sprang up. No, God provided in advance for mankind. God created light, heat, time, the land, and everything we would need first. He created all the air we would need to breathe, all the food we'd need to eat. He provided everything ahead of time.

When man first got hungry, God didn't have to say, "Oops, I forgot about that. Let me create a banana for you." No, God anticipated our needs. He created enough food to feed the entire world. There are over seven billion people on our planet today. Did you realize that there was enough food potential on this planet to feed all those people when there were only two? There was enough oxygen for seven billion people to breathe when there were only two. God created everything this world would ever need. He anticipated everything we could ever do to it and even thought through the necessary allowances that would help the planet deal with the effects of sin.

That's why I'm not a proponent of global warming and why I'm not worried about destroying the oceans or forests. Now, I love our planet. I love nature. I'm not advocating we intentionally mess things up. I believe we should be good stewards of everything the Lord has given us, including the earth. But our planet is not fragile. God has anticipated everything the human race could do to it. The earth is not going to be destroyed by us. Second Peter says the Lord has reserved judgment for the earth. He's going to destroy it with a fervent heat (2 Pet. 3:10). And as much as I hate breathing smog and think we should deal with the problem as good stewards, I also know that finite man isn't capable of overruling our infinite God.

Unfortunately, most Christians don't realize all that God provided for us. They constantly ask God to do something He's already done. They ask Him to give them something they already have. That's why their prayers aren't effective.

For example, many Christians read Galatians 2:20, which says we live by faith, but they miss the part that says our faith comes from God. And according to Romans 12:3, that faith is the same *"measure of faith"* that every person—even Jesus when He walked the earth—receives. Yet how many Christians pray, "God, give me more faith"? How can God answer a prayer like that? How can He give us more faith than He gave Jesus? We already have *the* measure of faith.

That's like a child sitting down to a Thanksgiving feast and asking "What's for dinner?" How would a person respond to such a question? I'd probably look at the child in silence and disbelief.

Maybe that's the reason you haven't heard from God. Maybe you're asking silly questions. Maybe you're praying silly prayers, prayers like "God, come. Meet with us in this place" or "God, go with us as we leave today." Hebrews 13:5 says He'll never leave us or forsake us. How can God answer prayers like that?

At this point, maybe you're thinking, *So, how do I pray? How do I know what to ask God?*

Ask according to the Word. First John says:

> *And this is the confidence that we have in him, that, if we ask any thing according to his will, he heareth us: And if we know that he hear us, whatsoever we ask, we know that we have the petitions that we desired of him.*

1 John 5:14-15

If you're praying what you see in the Word of God—specifically what you see in the New Testament after Jesus's death and resurrection—you can be confident you're praying in accordance with His will.

Take Paul's prayer in Ephesians and personalize it. That's what I did when I first got started. I said, "Father, open the eyes of my understanding. Help me direct my imagination to see the hope of Your calling. Help me know the exceeding greatness of Your power—the same power that raised Jesus from the dead—and the riches of the glory of Your inheritance that's in me." I guarantee that if you pray that prayer with a sincere heart, if you give God a chance, He will infuse your life with hope. He will cause your imagination to function positively. It may take a period of time, but the seed of God's Word will germinate in your heart. It will produce hope.

Hope—a positive imagination—changes the way you relate to life's circumstances. When sickness or poverty comes knocking on your door, you won't be intimidated. When depression and fear try to sneak in, hope will keep you safe. If you want to change, don't beg God to do what He's already done. Don't moan and groan to your friends and ask to be added to the prayer chain. Don't run around the country attending conferences so someone can "speak a word" over you or wave their hand and produce a miracle in your life. Change the way you think. Meditate on God's Word. See yourself the way He sees you. If you turn your imagination loose and get a clear picture of who you are and what you have in Christ, no devil in hell will be able to stop you. Satan and all his minions combined aren't strong enough to combat God's raising-from-the-dead power within you. They can't stop that picture from coming to pass!

Brothers and sisters, whether you need to see a miracle, desire new direction, or want to understand your new identity in Christ, you need to turn on your imagination. You have to see that picture of wholeness in your heart. Once you do, your life will be transformed, and you'll know the real power of your imagination.

RECEIVE JESUS AS YOUR SAVIOR

Choosing to receive Jesus Christ as your Lord and Savior is the most important decision you'll ever make!

God's Word promises that *"if thou shalt confess with thy mouth the Lord Jesus, and shalt believe in thine heart that God hath raised him from the dead, thou shalt be saved. For with the heart man believeth unto righteousness; and with the mouth confession is made unto salvation"* (Rom. 10:9-10). *"For whosoever shall call upon the name of the Lord shall be saved"* (Rom. 10:13).

By His grace, God has already done everything to provide salvation. Your part is simply to believe and receive.

Pray out loud, "Jesus, I confess that You are my Lord and Savior. I believe in my heart that God raised You from the dead. By faith in Your Word, I receive salvation now. Thank You for saving me!"

The very moment you commit your life to Jesus Christ, the truth of His Word instantly comes to pass in your spirit. Now that you're born again, there's a brand-new you!

Please contact our Helpline (719-635-1111) and let us know that you've prayed to receive Jesus as your Savior. We would like to rejoice with you and help you understand more fully what has taken place in your life. We'll send you a free gift that will help you understand and grow in your new relationship with the Lord. Welcome to your new life!

RECEIVE
THE HOLY SPIRIT

As His child, your loving heavenly Father wants to give you the supernatural power you need to live this new life.

> *For every one that asketh receiveth; and he that seeketh findeth; and to him that knocketh it shall be opened. . . . How much more shall your heavenly Father give the Holy Spirit to them that ask him?*

Luke 11:10 and 13b

All you have to do is ask, believe, and receive!

Pray, "Father, I recognize my need for Your power to live this new life. Please fill me with Your Holy Spirit. By faith, I receive it right now! Thank You for baptizing me. Holy Spirit, You are welcome in my life!"

Congratulations! Now you're filled with God's supernatural power!

Some syllables from a language you don't recognize will rise up from your heart to your mouth (1 Cor. 14:14). As you speak them out loud by faith, you're releasing God's power from within and building yourself up in your spirit (1 Cor. 14:4). You can do this whenever and wherever you like.

It doesn't really matter whether you felt anything or not when you prayed to receive the Lord and His Spirit. If you believed in your heart that you received, then God's Word promises that you did. *"Therefore I say unto you, What things soever ye desire, when ye pray, believe that ye receive them, and ye shall have them"* (Mark 11:24). God always honors His Word—believe it!

Please contact our Helpline (719-635-1111) and let us know that you've prayed to be filled with the Holy Spirit. We would like to rejoice with you and help you understand more fully what has taken place in your life. We'll send you a free gift that will help you understand and grow in your new relationship with the Lord.

ABOUT THE AUTHOR

Andrew Wommack's life was forever changed the moment he encountered the supernatural love of God on March 23, 1968. As a renowned Bible teacher and author, Andrew has made it his mission to change the way the world sees God.

Andrew's vision is to go as far and deep with the Gospel as possible. His message goes far through the *Gospel Truth* television program, which is available to nearly half the world's population. The message goes deep through discipleship at Charis Bible College, headquartered in Woodland Park, Colorado. Founded in 1994, Charis has campuses across the United States and around the globe.

Andrew also has an extensive library of teaching materials in print, audio, and video—most of which can be accessed for free from his website: **awmi.net**.

Contact Information

Andrew Wommack Ministries Inc.

PO Box 3333

Colorado Springs CO 80934-3333

Email: info@awmi.net

Helpline: 719-635-1111

Helpline Hours: 4:30 a.m. to 9:30 p.m. (MT)

awmi.net

FREE TEACHINGS

Andrew Wommack has a wealth of teaching materials just a click away! Watch a video, read a teaching article, or even download an audio teaching. From some of Andrew's early teachings to newer ones—covering a wide range of topics—**it's all available to you, completely free**!

Go to **awmi.net/popular** to start browsing today. Your life will never be the same!

Free Teachings

Welcome to Andrew's library of life-changing teachings! Whether you prefer to learn b, this page is sure to contain the answers you need from the Word of God.
Best of all, everything is offered to you at no cost. Why free teachings?

Relationship with God

Teaching Title	Video	Audio	Reading
The Effects of Praise	▶ Watch	🎧 Listen	📖 Read
The True Nature of God	▶ Watch	🎧 Listen	📖 Read
The War Is Over	▶ Watch	🎧 Listen	📖 Read
How to Hear God's Voice	▶ Watch	🎧 Listen	📖 Read

Grace

Teaching Title	
The Balance of Grace and Faith	
Grace: The Power of the Gospel	
The Power of Faith Filled Words	
Grace Encounters	

Healing

Teaching Title	Video	Audio	Reading
God Wants You Well	▶ Watch	🎧 Listen	📖 Read
You've Already Got It	▶ Watch	🎧 Listen	📖 Read
Better Way to Pray	▶ Watch	🎧 Listen	📖 Read
Healing Testimonies	▶ Watch		

Holy Spirit

Teaching Title
Spirit, Soul and Body
The New You
The Holy Spirit
Positive Ministry of the Holy

Finances

Teaching Title	Video	Audio	Reading
...dship	▶ Watch	🎧 Listen	📖 Read

Victorious

Teac...

 **awmi**.net

 ANDREW WOMMACK MINISTRIES

The Harrison House Vision

Proclaiming the truth and the power
of the Gospel of Jesus Christ with excellence.
Challenging Christians
to live victoriously,
grow spiritually,
know God intimately.

Connect with us on
f Facebook @ HarrisonHousePublishers
and **⊙** Instagram @ HarrisonHousePublishing
so you can stay up to date with news
about our books and our authors.

Visit us at **www.harrisonhouse.com**
for a complete product listing as well as
monthly specials for wholesale distribution.